The Qumran Hymns found among the famous Dead Sea Scrolls have revealed to us an impressive religious figure, previously unknown: the "Teacher of Righteousness." This mysterious spiritual leader has been hailed by some scholars as the Messiah and Redeemer. The important question is: will these discoveries change our understanding of Christ and His message? Using all the relevant Dead Sea Scrolls, Father Carmignac, a renowned scholar, has taken up the challenge of comparing the Teacher of Righteousness and Jesus Christ with respect to their persons and their works.

In a book written for the intelligent layman, Father Carmignac demonstrates that investigation into this delicate matter need cause no fear to Christian believers provided the *whole* body of evidence is examined. (All this material is presented for the reader's judgment in an Appendix.) Father Carmignac compares the two *persons* under investigation, discussing the subjects of Incarnation, Messiahship, Divinity, Crucifixion, and Second Coming. He then makes a comparison of their *works*: their Actions, Doctrines, the Sacraments, their Literary Expression and Thought.

Equally valuable to Christian minister, priest, and Jewish Rabbi, this book places in opposition "one of the most beautiful flowers in the garden of Jewish revelation"—a man who never applied to himself any Messianic trait—and the Founder of Christianity.

CHRIST
and the Teacher
of Righteousness

The Evidence of the
Dead Sea Scrolls

BY JEAN CARMIGNAC

Translated from the French
by Katharine Greenleaf Pedley

HELICON PRESS • BALTIMORE—DUBLIN

Helicon Press, Inc.
1120 N. Calvert Street
Baltimore 2, Maryland

Library of Congress Catalog Card Number 62-11183

Originally published in French, under the title *Le Docteur de Justice et Jésus-Christ* by Les Éditions de L'Orante, Paris.

Nihil Obstat: EDWARD A. CERNY, S.S., S.T.D.
Censor Librorum

Imprimature: ☩ LAWRENCE J. SHEHAN, D.D.
Archbishop of Baltimore
August 6, 1962

PRINTED IN THE UNITED STATES OF AMERICA BY

GARAMOND PRESS, BALTIMORE, MARYLAND

Foreword

ABBÉ CARMIGNAC's little book is easily the best of its kind. His good judgment is illustrated by his decision to provide documented and classified material which would enable intelligent readers to draw their own conclusions. As editor of the *Revue de Qumran,* which he founded four years ago, he has established a forum in which scholars of all faiths or none may contribute to the elucidation of the Dead Sea Scrolls in any of six languages.

Mrs. Pedley's translation from French is excellent, and the Abbé himself has assured accuracy by checking over it carefully. He has also encouraged the adaptation of the original to the needs of English readers by substituting a discussion of the writings of Charles F. Potter for the original treatment of equally derivative French writers in the second chapter. He has also added new material and references where particularly needed.

Abbé Carmignac's book is a beautiful example of the cooperative non-sectarian approach which distinguishes research on the Dead Sea Scrolls from most other publication in the wider biblical field. M. Carmignac is a Catholic secular priest; Mrs. Pedley is an Episcopalian;

I am a Methodist with Presbyterian leanings. Almost any scholarly position in the Qumran field will have Catholics, Jews and Protestants lined up both for and against it; doctrinal beliefs do not appreciably affect the philological and historical views of the protagonists. I say "appreciably" in order not to claim too much; actually I do not know of any case among scholars whom I consider "competent."

WILLIAM FOXWELL ALBRIGHT

Contents

FOREWORD by Dr. William Foxwell Albright . . . iii

TRANSLATOR'S PREFACE by Katharine G. Pedley . . vi

INTRODUCTION: The Discoveries at Qumran . . . 1

CHAPTER I: Did Jesus Imitate the Teacher of
Righteousness? 5

CHAPTER II: Christ and the Teacher Compared:
Their Persons 17

   1. Incarnation and Messiahship 17
   2. Divinity 32
   3. Passion and Crucifixion 48
   4. Resurrection and Second Coming 56
   5. Summary of All Texts Concerning the
     Teacher 66

CHAPTER III: Christ and the Teacher Compared:
Their Works and Doctrine 73

   1. Conduct 73
   2. Sacraments 66
   3. Doctrine 96
   4. Literary Expression 109

CHAPTER IV: The Teacher of Righteousness
Self-Revealed 115

CONCLUSION 127

APPENDIX: Texts From the Qumran Hymns . . . 133
   Explanatory Notes on the Hymns 155

BIBLIOGRAPHY 159

INDEX 165

Translator's Preface

IN ENGLAND and America there has been a flood of inexpensive and sensational books about the scrolls, with statements very alarming to the average reader· "The greatest challenge to Christian dogma since Darwin's theory of evolution," proclaims the cover of one fifty-cent paperback. The only American scholar who has taken public notice of some of these works is Dr. Millar Burrows, who says of one of them: "the interpretations offered are so far from anything even remotely suggested by the texts themselves that few scholars would consider it worth while to take time to refute them." Unfortunately, it is necessary to read some four hundred pages of his second volume on the scrolls to get all of his refutation; and the people likely to do this are not those who would have been bothered in the first place.

My delight was great, therefore, when I discovered that a French author, in *Le Docteur de Justice et Jesus-Christ*, had made a careful and scholarly rebuttal to certain books in the English language which had not previously been answered in that tongue, as well as to others by authors of unquestioned erudition but highly unorthodox belief. Abbé Carmignac's method is extremely simple. On each of the questions posed he quotes *all* the known texts from Qumran which are relevant, so that the reader can form a conclusion by the exercise of his own logical faculties. This has the added advantage of making reference to the material easy. The pertinent texts are found together, instead of being scattered here and there throughout the book (a literary device by which a small amount of matter can be made to loom very large). And he has not hesitated to repeat a text if it has bearing on more than one context, thereby minimizing the amount of "turning back" to verify references that is so often necessary.

Our collaboration started as a simple matter of translation, but as time went on, changes in the text were seen to be desirable and this book is now a thoroughly revised edition. New books in both languages kept appearing, and several of them required mention. Moreover, in 1961 the author published his complete translation of the *War Scroll* and the *Hymns* of Qumran (*Les Textes de Qumrân, traduits et annotés,* Paris, Letouzey et Ané) with critical introductions and extensive notes. Inevitably, he has made changes in his translation, and when he has done so we have adopted the newer reading for this book.

The entire translation has been carefully read by the author, who has urged me to keep it as free and idiomatic as possible. The translation of the *Hymns* was particularly difficult, since I had to render into English documents originally written in Hebrew. The author had set in italics all passages which were quotations from or echoes of the Old Testament, and for these I used the translation of the Revised Standard Version. The remainder of the text I tried to keep compatible with the style of that version. The reader should be warned that the numbering of certain passages—particularly the *Psalms*—is different in various versions. The references given in this book are to the Revised Standard Version, with foot-note references to other versions. The author is satisfied that I have translated his readings accurately.

The most able and eminent of the scholars with whom the Abbé Carmignac has found himself in disagreement is undoubtedly Professor André Dupont-Sommer, who was the first to champion the identification of the men of Qumran with the Essenes. While our book was in press, a new book by Dupont-Sommer was published simultaneously in England and the United States in a paperback edition. It should be said that he has been magnificently served by his brilliant translator, himself an almost equally eminent authority on the scrolls, and their translation of the Qumran texts is a literary classic. A careful comparison of this book with his earlier ones will show that in a surprising number of cases he has abandoned positions which Carmignac had shown to be untenable. This is naturally a matter of gratification for us, and we are happy to call attention to them. In some cases, however, Dupont-Sommer has substituted new and even more surprising theories for those abandoned, and we are glad that there has been time to include answers to these arguments before the final type was set.

A last word concerns the "Recommended Bibliography" appended to the book. In its original form it was prepared to accompany a lecture on the scrolls which I gave for a Library Association meeting in the spring of 1959, but it should be helpful to the general public as well. There are many different points of view represented, but the differences do not stem from denominational viewpoints. Practically all the authors listed would agree with the words the Abbé Carmignac wrote me as I commenced this translation: "The more I study these documents the more I am convinced that they are a precious support to the Christian faith." I am happy to have been privileged to play a small part in making this knowledge available to English-speaking readers.

The Discoveries at Qumran

I N THE spring of 1947 a Bedouin looking for a lost goat on the rocky cliff overhanging the Dead Sea near the Wadi Qumran found a cave containing some old rolls of parchment. Specialists who examined these manuscripts immediately saw that they represented what Dr. W. F. Albright, world-renowned archaeologist, called "the greatest manuscript discovery of modern times."

Bedouins and scholars inevitably followed up these discoveries, with the result that eleven caves have already yielded thousands upon thousands of fragments that are the vestiges of more than five hundred manuscripts. Archaeologists, in turn, undertook the excavation of some ruins that were visible between the cliffs and the Dead Sea, and exhumed the buildings of an ancient "monastery."[1]

All these discoveries naturally gave rise to heated controversy; but little by little the mystery has been cleared up and today scholars are almost all agreed that the manuscripts belong to the library of a community of Essenes[2]; that they were written between the end of the second century B.C. and the middle of the first century of

[1] See the valuable accounts given by Roland de Vaux, O.P., in *Revue Biblique*: (1953), No. 1, pp. 83–106; (1954), No. 2, pp. 206–36; (1956), No. 4, pp. 533–77: "Fouilles au Khirbet Qumrân."

[2] Dupont-Sommer deserves credit for having argued, from the very beginning, for the Essene origin of these manuscripts: see

1

the Christian era; and that they were hidden in the caves in A.D. 68 when the Essenes were attacked by the Romans.[3]

Although the editing of these rolls raised serious problems, all the contents of Cave I have now been published in photographic reproduction and in transcription. They consist of an entire manuscript of *Isaiah*, the complete text of the Rule of this community, a commentary (with gaps in the text) on the prophet *Habakkuk*,[4] another exemplar of *Isaiah*, the rule for *A War between the Sons of Light and the Sons of Darkness*, poetic meditations in the form of *Hymns*,[5] and a curious Aramaic paraphrase of *Genesis*.[6] Finally, there are some smaller fragments belonging to various Biblical texts and to a number of works, hitherto unknown for the most part, of which the best preserved are a *Rule of the Whole Congregation of Israel* and a collection of *Benedictions*.[7]

Observations sur le Commentaire d'Habacuc découvert près de la Mer Morte, pp. 26–28; *Aperçus Préliminaires sur les Manuscrits de la Mer Morte*, pp. 105–7 (English title, *The Dead Sea Scrolls; a Preliminary Survey*, pp. 86–89); *Nouveaux Aperçus sur les Manuscrits de la Mer Morte*, pp. 90–92, 96–104, etc. (English title, *The Jewish Sect of Qumran and the Essenes*, pp. 64–67, 70–74, etc.); "Les Esséniens," *Evidences*, No. 54 (January, 1956), pp. 19–22.

[3] Dupont-Sommer has also argued from the beginning for the date of this deposit which was afterwards accepted by the majority of scholars: "about A.D. 66–70" (*The Dead Sea Scrolls; a Preliminary Survey*, p. 23).

[4] These three manuscripts have been edited by Millar Burrows, *The Dead Sea Scrolls of St. Mark's Monastery*, Vol. I and Vol. II, fasc. 2.

[5] The fragments of these three works have been edited by E. L. Sukenik, *The Dead Sea Scrolls of the Hebrew University*.

[6] The passages actually deciphered have been edited by Nahman Avigad and Yigael Yadin, *A Genesis Apocryphon*.

[7] These various fragments have been edited by D. Barthélemy and J. T. Milik, *Discoveries in the Judaean Desert, I, Qumran Cave I.*

Caves II, III, V, and VI may have contained equally rich treasure, but the tatters of parchment or papyrus which have survived to our time are in a lamentable state. Even Cave IV has not yielded up a single complete work; but it has provided such an enormous number of fragments that the first indications, as reported by the scholars working on the decipherment, are extremely promising.[8]

Interest in these finds is immense. To begin with, we find ourselves in possession of very ancient Biblical manuscripts that are going to make possible the improvement of certain details in our editions of the Old Testament. The Hebrew text, transmitted from manuscript to manuscript, has inevitably suffered alterations in a number of minor points. As early as the period between the fifth and eighth centuries of our era a body of learned Jews called Masoretes had established the official text used down to the present time.

In order to improve on their work and approach more closely the original text the only sources we could formerly turn to were the ancient versions, or translations, of which the Greek Septuagint and the Syriac Peshitto are the most important. But now we find ourselves possessed of other evidence, more ancient than the Masoretic text and more faithful to the original than any of the versions. The comparison of these new data will entail an enormous amount of work; but they promise to throw most valuable light on many passages formerly more or less obscure.

Beyond and above this, we now have a first hand acquaintance with these Essenes, who together with the Sadducees and the Pharisees, influenced the life and thought of the Jewish people for more than a century

[8]See: "Le Travail d'édition des fragments manuscrits de Qumrân," *Revue Biblique*, (1956), No. 1, pp. 49–67. (English translation: "Editing the Manuscript Fragments from Qumran," *Biblical Archaeologist*, (1956), No. 4, pp. 75–96).

before the birth of Christ.[9] By reading their works, which possibly circulated in the hands of the hearers of the Gospel,[10] we can gain some insights into the mores and thought patterns to which Jesus may have adapted His message. We shall probably be able to learn in the future more exactly to what degree He was inspired by the ideas current around Him, and how far He approved, developed, corrected, or even condemned them.

In a way, a new era is opening up before the commentator and the historian of Christian origins. But immediately curiosity poses a question: Will these discoveries confirm or, on the contrary, will they change the understanding we have heretofore had of Christ and His message?

---

[9] Josephus, *Jewish Wars*, II, VIII, 2–13, 119–61; *Antiquities of the Jews*, XIII, V, 9, 171–73; XV, X, 4–5, 371–79; etc.

[10] This circulation of Essene works, however, must have been fairly limited, for it was strictly forbidden. Josephus tells us that the Essenes bound themselves by a mighty oath to keep secret both the books of their sect and the names of the angels. See *Jewish Wars*, II, VIII, 7, 142.

CHAPTER I

Did Jesus Imitate the
Teacher of Righteousness?

W HEN PUBLICATION of the Hebrew texts of these manuscripts began in April, 1950, A. Dupont-Sommer immediately discovered in them an interpretation so sensational that it threatened to jeopardize the fundamental originality of Christianity.

Basing his argument on passages that introduce a revered figure, the Teacher of Righteousness, he drew from them the conclusion that the spiritual superior and leader of the Essenes might well have served as inspiration to the earliest Christian community for the portrait it drew of its founder.

At least, these are the conclusions that Dupont-Sommer published in the summer of 1950:

[Essenism] in the last two centuries B.C. and the first century A.D. . . . represented a movement in Judaism as widespread as it was deep, both inside and outside Palestine. It is from the womb of this religious ferment that Christianity, the Christian "New Covenant," emerged. In history there are scarcely any absolute beginnings, and Christianity is no exception to the rule. Already eminent historians have recognized in Essenism a "foretaste of Christianity." This expression is one of Renan's, as also is: "Christianity is an Essenism which has largely succeeded." . . .

Everything in the Jewish New Covenant heralds and prepares the way for the Christian New Covenant. The Galilean Master, as He is presented to us in the writings of the New Testament, appears in many respects as an astonishing reincarnation of the Teacher of Righteousness. Like the latter He preached penitence, poverty, humility, love of one's neighbor, chastity. Like him, He prescribed the observance of the Law of Moses, the whole Law, but the Law finished and perfected, thanks to His own revelations. Like him He was the Elect and the Messiah of God, the Messiah redeemer of the world. Like him He was the object of the hostility of the priests, the party of the Sadducees. Like him He was condemned and put to death. Like him He pronounced judgment on Jerusalem, which was taken and destroyed by the Romans for having put Him to death. Like him, at the end of time, He will be the supreme judge. Like him He founded a Church whose adherents fervently awaited His glorious return. In the Christian Church, the essential rite is the sacred meal, whose ministers are the priests. Here and there at the head of each community there is the overseer, the "bishop." And the ideal of both Churches is essentially that of unity, communion in love—even going so far as the sharing of common property (*The Dead Sea Scrolls; a Preliminary Survey,* pp. 98-99).

All these similarities—and here I only touch upon the subject—together constitute a very impressive whole.[1]

After such a presentation many a reader has found himself asking: "Then what in the world did Jesus Christ have to offer? Why should the Son of God become incarnate if His only mission was to reproduce the example

---

[1] The various quotations from Dupont-Sommer are reproduced with his kind permission. Those that have been previously published in English translation are here reproduced in the same form, except that the phrase "Teacher of Righteousness" has been substituted for the less usual "Master of Justice" which Miss Rowley has used in her version of *Aperçus Préliminaires sur les Manuscrits de la Mer Morte,* quoted above (*Translator's note*).

given by the Teacher of Righteousness and to start the latter's work all over again?"

A heated argument naturally followed, and as a consequence two years later Dupont-Sommer was moved to give a further explanation of his real thinking:

Christianity is not Essenism, any more than Essenism is Christianity, or Christianity in anticipation. I, for my part, have never used any such formula, which would be an oversimplification of the problem. The sect of primitive Christians must in my view rather be ranked beside the sect of John the Baptist, among the many *quasi*-Essene sects which saw the light of Palestine in the course of the first century A.D. However important the borrowings may be which Christianity was able to make from Essenism properly speaking, Christianity is no copy or replica of Essenism. It is, to put it more exactly, a *quasi*-Essene neo-formation, the originality of which I am far from denying. It has no direct affiliations; as a neo-formation, it contains too much that is new to be considered as a repetition pure and simple. Christianity, I repeat, is not Essenism. It is, as Renan said, "*an* Essenism."

May I recall that in my previous book I summarized my views on this delicate subject thus: "Everything in the Jewish New Covenant heralds and prepares the way for the Christian New Covenant," and, quoting Renan, I referred to a "foretaste of Christianity." A heralding, a preparation, a foretaste: do not these words indicate that Christianity is the major fact, the creative originality of which no one thinks of denying? (*The Jewish Sect of Qumran and the Essenes*, p. 150)

In my desire to draw attention to this unexpected fact which the new texts seemed to disclose, I sketched out a rapid parallel which was intended to stimulate the curiosity of the reader, without pretending to solve a most complex problem at the price of over-simplification. If these few lines have contributed to stimulating research on this important point, they have served their purpose. . . .

Indeed, the resemblance is far from being complete. And that is why I took great care not to confound or identify the two personages with each other. On the contrary, I stressed that Jesus of Nazareth was another personage, "a new Prophet," "a new Messiah." To others who are distinguished experts in New Testament problems I must leave the task of determining in detail everything that makes for the originality of this "new prophet" and of the Church born out of faith in him. Suffice it here to point out that between the character of the Teacher of Righteousness and that of Jesus of Nazareth there are certain differences, which seem enough to remove all likelihood of Dr. Teicher's proposed identification being correct.[2]

The Teacher of Righteousness was a priest, a son of Levi; Jesus was not a priest, but "son of David." The Teacher of Righteousness was described as "Messiah of Aaron and Israel"[3]; Jesus was called only "the Messiah." The Teacher of Righteousness probably lived generally in Judaea; Jesus was a Galilean and His preaching took place principally on the shores of the Lake of Tiberias. The Teacher of Righteousness was a learned master, whom his followers surrounded with such a superstitious veneration that, like the disciples of Pythagoras, they would not pronounce his name; Jesus was a familiar teacher, whom His disciples and even the multitude approached with complete freedom, and whose name was neither secret nor mysterious. The Teacher of Righteousness, if one may judge by the quite monastic rule which he imposed on his followers, was a strict ascetic, no doubt charitable, but as hard on himself as on others, avoiding all contact with sinners like a pollution; Jesus mingled more with ordinary life, was more human. . . .

The Teacher of Righteousness was the revealer of a mysterious Gnostic teaching, which had been developed with the

[2] Dupont-Sommer here makes allusion to a theory proposed by J. L. Teicher, according to which the Teacher of Righteousness was Jesus Himself, and the community which produced the Qumran manuscripts would be quite simply a Christian community. This theory is rejected, with good reason, by most scholars.

[3] We shall see later, pp. 23–27, that this statement of Dupont-Sommer is debatable.

aid of the most profound wisdoms then in circulation in the world, and which was reserved to the initiated;[4] Jesus was, above all, a popular preacher, arisen from the circles of simple folk, who expressed himself in simple language with comparisons full of freshness and life. The Teacher of Righteousness was probably an author; the *Psalms* of Qumran and the *Manual of Discipline*[5] may have been partly composed by him. Jesus only preached, and wrote nothing. The Teacher of Righteousness was, to put it boldly, a kind of Jewish Pythagoras; Jesus, at least in the Synoptic Gospels, does not have this character at all. He was a simple soul, naïvely in love with the highest mystical ideals, who leaned naturally and warm heartedly towards God, without any learned theology, just as did later such a soul as Francis of Assisi (*The Jewish Sect of Qumrân and the Essenes*, pp. 160-62).

A few years later Dupont-Sommer returned to the same subject, and this time was able to use language even more reassuring to his Christian readers:

If it [the Essene sect] had the privilege of preparing the way, more than any other movement in Judaism, for the institution of Christianity, the originality of the latter, despite the affinities and the borrowings on which the new texts throw light, remains in its essence beyond our reach. But the historian of Christian origins sees the approaching dawn of the solutions of many problems and it is truly a new era that is opening before us in this realm of knowledge. Jesus and the new-born Christian church will be found to be rooted more solidly in history. Such a gain is of great value not only for the scholar, but doubtless also for those believers who are not indifferent to the earthly and human aspects of the Christian message (*Evidences*, No. 54 (January, 1956), p. 21).

[4] Many scholars do not think that the Teacher of Righteousness was so deeply influenced by foreign teachings; but on this point this is not the place to argue opinions with Dupont-Sommer.

[5] Dupont-Sommer, like many American scholars, uses this title for the *Rule of the Community*.

9

In brief, the more Dupont-Sommer pursued his meticulous study of the Qumran documents the more he toned down his emphasis on the ties between Essenism and Christianity and the greater importance he gave to the originality of the Christian revelation.[6]

One would have supposed further argument to be superfluous. Yet at the same time that this article appeared in the review *Evidences,* in January, 1956, one of the scholars who was working on the editing of the manuscripts from Cave IV, J. M. Allegro, was making an astounding broadcast on British television.

Here is the account of this performance given by *Time* magazine on February 6, 1956, p. 88, in a story entitled "Crucifixion before Christ":

According to Professor Allegro, [Alexander Jannaeus][7] was the man who descended on Qumran and arrested its leader, the mysterious "Teacher of Righteousness," whom he turned over to his mercenaries to be crucified.

"Already, in Jerusalem, this Jewish tyrant had displayed his bestiality by inflicting the same awful death on eight hundred rebels," says Professor Allegro. "A Qumran manuscript speaks in shocked tones of the enormity of this crime. . . .

[6] Later Dupont-Sommer still further explained his actual thinking: "It would be a mistake, we think, to make an argument from these affinities and resemblances, no matter how remarkable and convincing they may appear, either to make of the Gospel narratives a simple retelling of the story of the Teacher of Righteousness, a pure fiction in which Jesus would be only a mythological doublet of the Essene prophet, or to identify the Teacher of Righteousness, as some have tried to do, with Jesus Himself . . ." (*Les écrits esséniens découverts près de la Mer Morte* [Paris, 1959], p. 385).

[7] From 103 to 76 B.C. Alexander Jannaeus exercised the functions both of High Priest and King of the Jews. Because of his vices and his cruelty, many scholars believe that he may have been the "Wicked Priest" or the "Lion of Fury" mentioned in the Qumran documents. On this point Allegro's hypothesis is entirely possible; still it is only a hypothesis.

"When the Jewish king had left, the community took down the broken body of their Master to stand guard over it until Judgment Day. For they believed that the terrible events of their time were surely heralding the visitation of God Himself, when the Kingdom of Heaven would come in. . . . They believed their Master would rise again and lead his faithful flock (the people of the new testament as they called themselves) to a new and purified Jerusalem."

The Qumran community looked for the coming of two Messiahs—their own Teacher and a Messiah from the line of David. "At one time it was all so clear, but now everything seems to be in the melting pot. What is clear is that there was a well-defined Essenic[8] pattern into which Jesus of Nazareth fits. What the theologians make of that is really outside my province. I just give my findings."

Such words, when supposedly backed up by texts not yet edited, could hardly fail to cause enormous repercussions.

Later, in the course of the same year, 1956, Allegro published a book entitled *The Dead Sea Scrolls*, in which he developed the same theories more fully. He took care, to be sure, not to express them in so categorical a fashion; but the general orientation of his narrative and the many expressions scattered skillfully throughout the whole work, give the impression that he always considers the life of Jesus as a kind of legend inspired by the example of the Teacher of Righteousness:

For the early Jewish-Christian Church an "objective" life of Jesus would have been as pointless as one of the Teacher for the Qumran Community (*The Dead Sea Scrolls*, p. 133).

Journalists were naturally interested in so serious a question; and so we may count by hundreds the articles—

[8] Quoting this phrase in *The Times* (London), March 20, 1956, p. 13, Allegro wrote "Messianic pattern" and not "Essenic pattern."

11

some with and some without adequate documentation—whose authors have sought to popularize the conclusions of scholarly studies.

In the United States and England excellent works have been published by qualified scholars. Readers desiring serious information will be amply rewarded by Frank M. Cross' book, *The Ancient Library of Qumran and Modern Biblical Studies* (1958) and the more recent work of Edmund F. Sutcliffe, S.J., *The Monks of Qumran*. The fullest treatment is found in the two large works of Millar Burrows, *The Dead Sea Scrolls* (1955) and *More Light on the Dead Sea Scrolls* (1958); while those more pressed for time will find a judicious appraisal in *A Guide to the Scrolls*, by Leaney–Posen–Hanson (London, 1958).

But the English-speaking public has been deluged also by other works that have not the same scholarly value.

The critic and reporter, Edmund Wilson, although he made a laudable effort to inform himself on the subjects of which he wrote, was above all concerned to give his recital "the fascination and high drama of a detective story" (see cover of his Fontana Books edition), and he sometimes allowed his fondness for brilliant writing to run away with him to the point where he would have had considerable trouble proving his thesis as, for example, when he wrote:

The monastery, this structure of stone that endures between the bitter waters and precipitous cliffs, with its oven and its inkwells, its mill and its cesspools, its constellation of sacred fonts and the unadorned graves of its dead, is perhaps, more than Bethlehem or Nazareth, the cradle of Christianity (*The Dead Sea Scrolls*, Oxford Press ed., pp. 97-98. Fontana Books ed. p. 104).

A. Powell Davies was another of the popularizers. His

work, *The Meaning of the Dead Sea Scrolls*, begins by giving a reliable account of the manuscripts, their discovery and dating (pp. 9-42); but then, intsead of studying objectively the contents of these writings, he builds up a vast synthesis, purely imaginative, which rests on no proof and is worth no more than dreams. From time to time he takes care to mention the conjectural character of his constructions: *e.g.*, "even though we are dealing only with hypothesis" (p. 109); "none of the above is set forth as assured exegesis. All that is intended is the application of our new insights to events that may become more meaningful if we can learn to see them in a clearer context" (pp. 113-114). But many readers are likely to forget these prudent reservations and to believe that the proposed conclusions are based on solid arguments.

In reality, the author is content to repeat, in one form after another, his fundamental propositions: "It seems more and more possible that at the beginning Essenic Judaism and Palestinian Christianity were one and the same plant" (p. 105) . . . "We see the strong probability that his [Jesus'] education was Essene, and as we know from previous sections, his teaching and his entire outlook relate him to the Essenes" (p. 111).

Charles Francis Potter, whose publisher has proclaimed him to be a "world-renowned religious leader and scholar," has produced a book, *The Lost Years of Jesus Revealed*, which is advertised on its front cover as the "newest revelations of the Dead Sea Scrolls," but which contains, on the contrary, not a single new text and very little reliable information. With imperturbable self-assurance the author sets forth his own personal theories, doubtless hoping that naïve readers will accept his affirmations as proven facts:

Surely with the evidence at hand, any fair-minded Christian should admit that Jesus was not a miraculous incarnation of a Son of God, pre-existent in the heavens and sent to earth as the long-awaited Messiah, to suffer and die on the cross for the sins of Adam and all Adam's children. . . . Rather, the personality of Jesus was the remarkable but natural product, outgrowth, flowering, and fruiting of the living, thinking, suffering, and teaching of many generations of Hebrew prophets, law-givers, priests and students, religious leaders and ethical teachers (*Ibid.*, p. 40).

As scroll after scroll is unrolled and bushels of priceless fragments are sorted and deciphered, it is seen more and more clearly how much this strange unnamed Man of Destiny, the Teacher of Righteousness, resembled in many ways the man Jesus, while at the same time he differed so much from the Christ-God of the later theologians. . . .

In the light of these Scrolls, their contents and particularly their pre-Christian origin, there must take place a radical and thorough review, restudy, and revaluation of extremely important matters such as the education, beliefs, parentage, deity, and even the existence of the unusual person named Jesus, called Christ, together with the related problems of the origin, founders, liturgy, doctrines, and early literature of the Christian Church. . . .

It may be that this Qumran leader's brief biography, with additional items we have not yet discovered, became the literary foundation of Christianity. That seems improbable, but the possibility must be carefully explored. It is more likely that Jesus, who was evidently very familiar with the books of the Qumran library, patterned his own career and teachings in part after this great religious leader, teacher, and martyr (*Ibid.*, pp. 120-21).

Unfortunately, we look in vain through the entire work for a scholarly argument that would demonstrate with any certainty such important "revelations."

In short, many publications have tried too soon to inform the general public concerning hypotheses that have not yet been submitted to sufficient scientific examination. And the general public has obviously forgotten the provisional character of these hypotheses and regards them almost as authoritative disclosures.

Here, for example, is the comment of an American traveler encountered by chance: "You know, Jesus Christ never existed! They have found some old manuscripts near the Dead Sea that show that He never lived and that someone else lived in His place."

So we must ask the authors who have, doubtless unconsciously, provoked such reactions in the general public, to forgive those who are obliged to take up this discussion in detail in order to aid the non-specialist to form a more complete, a more balanced, and, we hope, a more correct opinion on this vital issue.

Christ and the Teacher Compared: Their Persons

1. Incarnation and Messiahship

IF IT is our purpose to throw as much light as possible on this discussion, we cannot be satisfied with merely piling up all the conspicuous similarities between the Teacher of Righteousness and Jesus, but rather we must analyze these similarities one by one in order to determine more clearly the meaning of the texts. Only then shall we be in a position to see how the relation between the Founder of the Christian Church and the principal Teacher of Essenism can and ought to be evaluated.

The first resemblance alleged is that each is an incarnation of Divinity. *The Habakkuk Commentary* contains the following clause:

And odious profaners committed horrors on him [the Teacher of Righteousness] and vengeance on his body of flesh.[1]

Now here is the explanation that Dupont-Sommer gives of this passage: "If the commentator speaks of his 'body of flesh' does it not mean that he considers that the

---

[1] A number of translators understand this differently, but in order to avoid argument we adopt without quibble the translation of Dupont-Sommer.

Teacher, being of divine nature, has literally 'become flesh'?" (*Revue de l'Histoire des Religions*, 137 [April-June, 1950], p. 164). Then later he amplifies his statement: "He [the Teacher of Righteousness] suffered in 'his body of flesh': without doubt he was a divine being who 'became flesh' to live and die as a man" (*The Dead Sea Scrolls; a Preliminary Survey*, p. 34).

Later on Professor Étiemble, one of the popularizers of Dupont-Sommer, was led to intensify even more strongly this last formula: "This is in all likelihood a question of a divine being who became flesh 'to live and die *as man*' " (*Temps Modernes*, January, 1951, p. 1288, italics added by the translator).

Such an exegesis, of course, aroused lively protest. To say that someone has a body of flesh does not imply that he existed before having this body—and then that he has a divine nature—and then that he has become incarnate in order to live as a man.

The expression "body of flesh" is found in other ancient texts and it always keeps its normal meaning, which is to insist on the physical reality of a body, just as we say "flesh and blood." Thus:

The profligate, in his body of flesh, finds no repose (*Ecclus.* 23:17. Greek version only).

And you . . . he has now reconciled in his body of flesh by his death . . . (*Col.* 1:22).

In him also you are circumcised with a circumcision made without hands, by putting off the body of flesh in the circumcision of Christ (*Col.* 2:11).

And grieve not if your soul into Sheol has descended in grief, and that in your life your body fared not according to your goodness (*Enoch*, CII, 5, trans. by R. H. Charles).[2]

[2] These texts have been brought together with critical comment by M. Philonenko, "Sur l'expression 'Corps de Chair' dans le Commentaire d'Habakuk," *Semitica*, V, pp. 39–40.

Quite otherwise than Dupont-Sommer, who spoke thus of "the incarnation" of the Teacher of Righteousness, Potter affirms again and again his skepticism concerning the incarnation of Christ (see pages 15, 41 ff., and elsewhere). But, as usual, he brings forth no argument to support his allegations. It is hard to see what argument he could produce or how the texts of Qumran could raise a question concerning the incarnation of Christ, since these texts were composed before the time of Christ, and Potter is in full agreement as to "their pre-Christian origin" (*The Lost Years of Jesus Revealed*, p. 121).

The second alleged resemblance concerns Messiahship.[3] The messianic character of the Teacher of Righteousness is affirmed with such insistence by Dupont-Sommer and Allegro[4] that we may content ourselves with citing only a few of their statements:

This title of "Anointed One"—that is to say "Messiah" or "Christ"—deserves special attention. . . . In the *Damascus Document*[5] the messianic quality of the Teacher is altogether explicit.[6]

Such, according to the evidence of the Dead Sea documents, is the unexpected history of the Teacher of Righteousness,

[3] The proper word here is *messiahship* and not *messianism*. This study does not deal with the *messianism* at *Qumran* but with the *messiahship of the Teacher of Righteousness*.

[4] And equally by other authors; thus M. R. Goosens entitled one of his articles, "Onias le Juste, le Messie de la Nouvelle Alliance, lapidé à Jerusalem en 65 avant Jesus Christ" (*La Nouvelle Clio*, No. 7 [July, 1950], pp. 336–53).

[5] This previously known work is also called the *Zadokite Fragments* or the *Zadokite Document* by a number of English authors, and is also sometimes referred to as the *Cairo Document*.

[6] Dupont-Sommer, *The Dead Sea Scrolls; a Preliminary Survey*, pp. 63–64. Five years later Dupont-Sommer expressed himself in a less positive fashion: "The *Damascus Document*, where I continue to see allusions to the messianic character of the Teacher" . . . (*Vetus Testamentum*, No. 2, [1955], p. 120).

Elect of God and Messiah of God (Dupont-Sommer, *Revue de Paris*, August, 1951, p. 104).

Yes, for his devotees the Teacher of Righteousness became a Prophet and a Messiah (*The Jewish Sect of Qumran and the Essenes*, p. 55).

The Priest-Messiah, the Messiah of Aaron, that is to say the Priest who founded the sect and whom his faithful called the Teacher of Righteousness (*Evidences*, No. 56 [April, 1956], p. 17).

The mysterious Teacher of Righteousness, this priestly Messiah . . . (*Ibid.*, p. 25, and *Encyclopédie Française*, 19, 42-44).

The Priest . . . is the Messiah of Aaron, the Priest-Messiah; he is, according to us, the Teacher of Righteousness himself (*Evidences*, No. 57 [May, 1956], p. 11).

The Qumran Sect looked to the coming of a Priestly Messiah, whom they called 'Teacher of Righteousness' . . . (Allegro, *The Dead Sea Scrolls*, p. 148).

Their messianic Teacher of Righteousness . . . (*Ibid.*, p. 149).

In fact, the term *mashiah*—which has given us the English "Messiah"—is employed some ten times among the texts actually published. But we should begin by pointing out that the Aramaic and Hebrew terms and the European derivative do not always have an identical meaning. For us the word "Messiah" (or its Greek translation, "Christos") designates the Savior sent by God for the redemption of the world,[7] whereas in the Hebrew this word keeps its etymological meaning of "anointed" or "consecrated" and can be applied, according to circumstances, to those who have received priestly unction, kingly unction, prophetic unction, or unction pure and simple—messianic and reserved for the future Savior of the people.

[7] Dupont-Sommer is in complete agreement on this point, which he makes exquisitely precise: "The Messiah of God, the Messiah Redeemer of the world" (see above, p. 6).

If we review all the known occurrences of the word *mashiah* at Qumran, and adopt provisionally the wide meaning of "anointed," letting the context determine the meaning, we find that in three cases the prophetic unction is clearly meant:[8]

Through the agency of Thine anointed ones, the seers of the evidence, Thou hast told us the times of the wars of Thy hands (*War Scroll*, XI, 7-8).

He (God) instructed them (of old time) through the agency of the anointed ones of His Spirit of holiness and of the seers of the Truth (*Damascus Document*, II, 12-13).[9]

The commandments of God handed down through the agency of Moses and also by the anointed ones of holiness (*Ibid.*, V, 21–VI, 1).[10]

In one case the kingly unction is obviously meant:

When there shall be dominion for Israel [there will not] be cut off a king in it belonging to David. For the *ruler's staff* is the royal mandate . . . *until* the anointed one of righteousness *shall come*, the shoot of David, for to him and to his seed has been given the royal mandate over his people for everlasting generations . . . (*Genesis Commentary*, text published by Allegro, "Further Messianic References in Qumran Literature," *Journal of Biblical Literature*, No. 3 [1956], pp. 174–75).

[8] Dupont-Sommer is again in perfect agreement on this point. Concerning the first text he says, "The 'Anointed ones,' gifted with supernatural prescience, are here the Prophets," (*Revue de l'Histoire des Religions*, 148 [October–December, 1955], p. 160); concerning the second, "The 'Anointed ones' are here the Prophets who, down through the ages, have passed on to the elect the divine revelations" (*Evidences*, No. 59 [August, 1956], p. 24, note 19); concerning the third, "The Prophets," (*op. cit.*, p. 26, note 66).

[9] We have adapted here the excellent reading suggested by Dupont-Sommer (*Evidences*, No. 59 [August, 1956], p. 24, note 19) and taken over by Y. Yadin (*Israel Exploration Journal*, No. 3 [1956], pp. 158–59).

[10] We follow a new (and happy) correction of Dupont-Sommer.

The other six times there is nothing to prove that this is the peculiarly messianic unction conferring the role of Savior:

In the time of wickedness, until the anointed of Aaron and Israel shall arise (*Damascus Document*, XII, 23–XIII, 1).

Aaron and Israel . . . [These words are preceded by a letter which could be the last of "anointed." The text is defective.] (*Ibid.*, XIV, 19).

They shall be delivered up to the sword upon the coming of the anointed one of Aaron and Israel (*Ibid.*, XIX, 10–11).

From the day of the disappearance of the Teacher of the Community[11] until there shall arise the anointed [issue] of Aaron and [issue] of Israel . . . (*Ibid.*, XIX, 35–XX, 1).

They shall be ruled according to the first regulations to which the men of the community began to conform, until there shall come a prophet and the anointed ones of Aaron and Israel (*Rule of the Community*, IX, 10–11).

If (God) brings to birth among them the anointed one[12] . . . Afterwards shall the anointed of Israel be seated . . . Afterwards shall the anointed of Israel place his hand on the bread (*Rule for the Whole Congregation of Israel*, II, 12, 14, 20).

In an unknown liturgical text there is one mention of "the anointed one of holiness" (*Qumran Cave I*, No. 30, p. 132). Unfortunately, in the absence of any context to clarify the sense of this passage, it cannot help us.

---

[11] The careless scribe of the *Damascus Document* wrote "Teacher of the Only." This is generally corrected to "the Only Teacher" (Dupont-Sommer) or "Teacher of the Community" (Vermes); in any case the Teacher of Righteousness is meant.

[12] Dr. Yigael Yadin, a former chief of state and major in the Israeli Army, and now a professor at the Hebrew University in Jerusalem, has recently proposed another reconstruction of this passage: "On the occasion of their meeting, the anointed priest will come with them . . . " (*Journal of Biblical Literature*, September, 1959, pp. 238–41).

Thus there is no one certain translation of this passage. "The anointed" of Aaron could very well be in reality the high priest and "the anointed" of Israel the head of the state, the one having received the priestly unction and the other the kingly; thus our texts would show only the expectation of the prophet, the high priest, and the king who were to preside at the inauguration of the reign of God on earth.

But, since all this explanation is not certain, let us see what follows if we assume that in these six passages the term "anointed" might apply to the "Messiah redeemer of the world." The forms used in the *Rule of the Community* and the *Rule for the Whole Congregation of Israel* show that two "Messiahs" were looked for—the one a descendent of Aaron and the other, of Israel. The more equivocal formulation of the *Damascus Document* ought, then, to be interpreted in the same way: "the Messiah of Aaron and Israel" meaning "the Messiah of Aaron and (the one) of Israel"—as is normal in Hebrew, which has no pronoun equivalent to "the one."[13]

In spite, however, of the altogether explicit parallels in the *Rule of the Community* and the *Rule for the Whole Congregation of Israel,* suppose we concede further to Dupont-Sommer the right to maintain that the *Damascus Document* recognized but one "Messiah" only, descended both from Aaron and from Israel. Even then an impediment remains. Of all the Qumran texts known so far which mention the term *mashiah,* nine out of ten (or ten out of eleven if we count the *Liturgical Text*) do not mention the Teacher of Righteousness; and the one that does (*Damascus Document,* XX, 1) mentions him in order to differentiate, to the point of opposition, between

[13] Similarly in popular speech "a quart of wine and water" could mean "a quart each of wine and water" or "a quart of wine mixed with water."

"Teacher of Righteousness" and the "Messiah(s)," as we see from the words themselves:

From the day of the disappearance of the Teacher of the Community until there shall arise the Messiah (?) [issue] of Aaron and [the one?] [issue] of Israel.

Under these circumstances, does it not seem unwarranted to affirm so often that the men of Qumran believed the Teacher of Righteousness to be the "Messiah"?

To be sure, Dupont-Sommer has tried to answer this argument. Here is the gloss with which he accompanies this text from the *Damascus Document*:

"The anointed issue of Aaron and of Israel" is identical—we say it emphatically—with the "Teacher of Righteousness"; this is the Anointed One, the Messiah. If the author varies his terms, this simply arises from the most elementary rhetoric (*Revue de l'Histoire des Religions*, 137 [April-June, 1950], 161, note 1).

Is it so difficult to imagine that, in the passage quoted, its author should have used two different expressions to indicate one and the same person? Such a practice is a feature of the most elementary rhetoric (*Jewish Sect of Qumrân and the Essenes*, p. 55).

We must admit that Dupont-Sommer's appeal to the most elementary rhetoric leaves us unconvinced. Look at the text again: "From the day of the disappearance of the Teacher of the Community until there shall arise the Messiah [issue] of Aaron and [the one?] [issue] of Israel." Can this really mean, "From the disappearance[14] of the Teacher of Righteousness until the appearance of the Teacher of Righteousness"? And this is the only text that

[14] This "disappearance" is, of course, generally accepted as meaning the death of the Teacher of Righteousness.

would suggest the messiahship of the Teacher of Right-eousness![15]

Since this refutation was first published in France in November 1957 Dupont-Sommer's ideas seem to have undergone a surprising evolution: the men of Qumran now turn out to have had no one doctrine about the eschatological role of their Teacher of Righteousness, but saw him rather as playing various parts from one document to another. Thus, in the most recent of his works, *The Essene Writings from Qumran*, 1962 (French edition, *Les écrits esséniens découverts près de la Mer Morte*, 1959) Dupont-Sommer tells us (page 50) that a text of the *Rule of the Congregation* (called by him the *Rule Annexe*)

describes the ideal Supper, the Supper over which the Priest and the Messiah of Israel will preside at the end of time—the latter being clearly subordinate to the former. Now the Priest in question here is the Priest-Messiah, the Messiah of Aaron, the Priest, that is to say, who founded the sect and was known to its members as the 'Teacher of Righteousness'. Although this Teacher suffered and was put to death, he still lived, and his followers expected him to return at the end of time with the Messiah of Israel, the King-Messiah. The Supper which the members of the New Covenant celebrated each day referred essentially to the Supper which would take place later when the Kingdom of God had come. The humble daily supper was therefore a constant reminder of the revered

---

[15] Let no one object that this messiahship could itself be referred to under varying terms; for such a statement could hardly have meaning except for such expressions as "elect of God", which will be considered on pp. 61–63, or "shoot of David" which designates a warrior Messiah very different from the Christian one and which has never yet been applied to the Teacher of Righteousness. (See Allegro, "Further Messianic References in Qumran Literature," *Journal of Biblical Literature*, 3[1956], pp. 174–87.)

Teacher, and the presiding priest was, so to speak, the representative of, or substitute for, the Priest *par excellence.*

A little later (page 94) we learn that in the *Rule of the Community*

the expression . . . 'until the coming of the Prophet and the Anointed of Aaron and Israel' suggests that the Prophet's appearance, and the subsequent inauguration of the eschatological era, would be followed after a fairly brief delay by the coming of the two Anointed of Aaron and Israel (the Priest-Messiah and the King-Messiah). This passage from the *Rule* seems to infer that the eschatological age had begun and that the Prophet had already appeared. For the sectaries of the Covenant, however, this prophet could scarcely be anyone but the Teacher of Righteousness himself. It nevertheless seems that *in this passage* the Teacher is identified as the Prophet, but not yet as the Priest-Messiah, as he will be later. (See *supra.*)

Still later, commenting on the *Damascus Document* (page 139) he tells us that

'The Unique Teacher' is the Teacher of Righteousness, the sect's founder and lawgiver. He is dead but will return again at the end of time . . . Here there is the question of the coming of the 'Messiah sprung from Aaron and Israel'; in my view there is nothing to contradict the identification of this Messiah with the Teacher of Righteousness himself, reappearing at the end of time.

Finally (page 138f) he states his present position very plainly:

The messianic beliefs of the Qumran sect are really very complex; they did not remain fixed and immutable for centuries. In fact they appear in the Qumran texts in a variety of forms testifying to numerous experiments and considerable evolution. Although the Teacher of Righteousness was *at times* (italics his) considered the one complete Messiah, the 'Anointed of

Aaron and Israel', *at others* he was, I think, recognized as the sacerdotal Messiah only—the office of lay Messiah, King-Messiah, being then relegated to a person still to come. In a matter such as this, there was room for speculation of every sort within the Essene sect, speculation which varied according to circumstances and according to the inspiration of their great prophets and doctors.

To statements as self-contradictory as these, what scholarly worth can be accorded? On the evidence, the Qumran sectaries could have had no very certain "faith" in their Teacher of Righteousness. But we have just seen that the study of the texts shows that nowhere is the Teacher identified either with the Messiah of Aaron or the Messiah of Israel. Dupont-Sommer tells us that "there is nothing to contradict the identification of this Messiah (sprung from Aaron and Israel) with the Teacher of Righteousness himself." It could be argued that some of the Dead Sea texts themselves contradict this identification by the author's own admission, but it seems unnecessary. For the historian it is not enough to say that "nothing contradicts . . ." Surely a positive argument is needed, based on at least one text.

Nevertheless, Dupont-Sommer proposes still another argument, one that he finds in a work known to us previously only in Greek, *The Testaments of the Twelve Patriarchs.* Here is the outline of his reasoning:

The *Testaments of the Twelve Patriarchs* (is) an incomparable mine for the understanding of the doctrines of the Jewish sect of the New Covenant . . . In particular, an abundant harvest of texts relative to the dead and glorified Anointed One is to be found there, a whole "Christology" developed at length, a whole "mystery of salvation" perfectly elaborated. There can be no doubt that this Anointed One was the Teacher of Righteousness who founded the New Covenant.

27

Hitherto perplexed exegetes faced with such texts have usually found in them the interpolations of Christian copyists. But now that there is positive information about the actual historical existence of a Messiah[16] who suffered and died under Aristobulus II, thanks to the *Habakkuk Commentary*, such excisions which could formerly be understood are now no longer to be tolerated; these "Christological" passages, taken as a whole, henceforth seem to be of the greatest worth, and to continue to reject them *a priori* as being of Christian origin would appear to be contrary to all sound method. It is now certain—and this is one of the most important revelations of the Dead Sea discoveries—that Judaism in the first century B.C. saw a whole theology of the suffering Messiah, of a Messiah who should be the redeemer of the world, developing around the person of the Teacher of Righteousness (*The Dead Sea Scrolls; a Preliminary Survey*, pp. 95–96).

This argument seemed to Dupont-Sommer so important that he developed it at length in a special article, "Le Testament de Lévi (XVII-XVIII) et la Secte Juive de l'Alliance," *Semitica*, IV, 33–53, and took up the study again in a chapter of *The Jewish Sect of Qumran and the Essenes*, pp. 38–57. In fact, when he drafted these pages in 1950 and 1952, his reasoning still seemed cogent. But at present it has lost its probability.

Since the close of the last century a few Hebrew or Aramaic fragments of the *Testaments of the Twelve Patriarchs* have been known,[17] and the caves of Qumran have

---

[16] Dupont-Sommer should be reminded that the *Habakkuk Commentary* never refers explicitly to the "Messiah."

[17] Gaster, "The Hebrew Text of one of the Testaments of the Twelve Patriarchs," *Proceedings of the Society of Biblical Archaeology*, XVI [1893-94], 33–49 and 109–117; Pass-Arendzen, "Fragment of an Aramaic Text of the Testament of Levi," *Jewish Quarterly Review*, XII [1899-1900], 651–61; Charles-Cowley, "An Early Source of the Testaments of the Patriarchs," same review, XIX [1906-07] 566–83; Charles, *The Greek Versions of the Testaments of the Twelve Patriarchs*, pp. 245–56, (1908); Charles, *The Apoc-*

just turned up several more (J. T. Milik, *Qumran Cave I,* No. 21, (1955) pp. 87-91; *Ibid.,* "Le Testament de Lévi en araméen, Fragment de la Grotte 4 de Qumrân," *Revue Biblique,* (1956), No. 3, pp. 391-406). Both by direct study of the Greek text (De Jonge, *The Testaments of the Twelve Patriarchs,* 1953) and by comparison of the Aramaic and the Greek (P. Grelot, "Notes sur le Testament araméen de Lévi," *Revue Biblique,* No. 3, (1956), pp. 391-406), scholars have arrived at the conclusion that the *Testaments* in Hebrew or Aramaic and the Greek *Testaments* are two separate works, one composed by an Essene and the other by a Christian. The Greek work might have been inspired by the Semitic *Testaments*—or more probably by another work which may have been the source of both[18]—but its author actually "wrote a new Christian

---

rypha and Pseudepigrapha of the Old Testament in English," II, 361–67 (1913) . . .

In Gaster's opinion: "In comparing (the Hebrew text) with the Greek version, we are struck by the great disparity between the two. In the Hebrew version whole chapters of the Greek are missing, whilst in the Greek, the whole of the Hebrew is condensed into four and a half chapters and the contents mangled almost beyond recognition" (p. 42). And according to Pass-Arendzen: "The discovery of the Armenian version has placed it beyond doubt that the author of our Greek text handled his material with considerable freedom, both omitting from, adding to, and re-moulding the original text. It was therefore to be expected that the Aramaic text would show some considerable divergence from the Greek, and this will be seen to be the case, although their verbal identity in many places is an almost certain testimony to their common origin" (p. 652).

[18] "We cannot even say without qualification that the Greek *Testament* derives directly from the Aramaic text. . . . De Jonge does not try to trace the Greek directly to a Hebrew original; he thinks both Greek and Aramaic have evolved in parallel fashion from a single Aramaic prototype, but that ultimately this in its turn must have derived from a Hebrew text" (P. Grelot, *Revue Biblique,* No. 3 [1956], pp. 404 and 406).

Testament" (De Jonge, *op. cit.,* p. 52). His work may serve to throw light on the "social and religious life of the early Christian Church," but it "can no longer be used to illustrate the preparation of Christianity" (*Ibid.,* p. 128).

Certainly, the problem of the origin and composition of the *Testaments of the Twelve Patriarchs* is not yet resolved. On the one hand, an undeniable relation between this work and the texts of Qumran has been demonstrated; but on the other hand, the work contains doctrines absolutely foreign, or even opposed to, the thinking of the men of Qumran. Thus, the passages referring to the ruin of Jerusalem and of the Temple (*Levi,* X, 3; XVI, 4; *Benjamin,* IX, 4), of the resurrection of the dead (*Benjamin,* X, 7-8), and especially of the incarnation of the Savior (*Simeon,* VI, 5-7; VII, 2; *Nephtali,* VIII, 3; *Benjamin,* X, 7-8) are incompatible with the Qumran texts so far known. Under these circumstances, no one can affirm absolutely that *all* the content of the *Testaments* comes from Qumran, and no one can yet distinguish clearly between the Essene and the Christian elements that are mingled in this work. Consequently, in the present state of our knowledge, no valid arguments can be constructed on so uncertain a base.

But Dupont-Sommer has yet another round of ammunition to fire. In *The Essene Writings from Qumran,* p. 364 (French text p. 375), he sees in the Teacher of Righteousness "the replica of that Man of Sorrows whose tragic destiny, and whose valour in the face of blows and final exaltation are described in the fourth 'Servant Song' (*Isa.* 53:12)." He therefore supposes that a redemptive value should be attributed to the Teacher's sufferings. Once again, we must examine the texts, looking not for what we should like to find in them but for what they do actually say. 637 quotations from the Old Testament have been identified in the *Hymns;* but only six of them are

30

from the Servant[19] poems, and these say nothing of significance for us: "nothing and vanity" (*Isa.* 49:4); "a time of favor" (*Isa.* 49:8); "I clothe the heavens in somber hues"[20] (*Isa.* 50:3); "at tongue of instruction"[21] (*Isa.* 50:4); "to sustain with a word him that is weary" (*Isa.* 50:4); and "we esteemed him not" (*Isa.* 53:3).

How can we, on the basis of these sole texts, imagine that the Servant poems exercised a profound influence on the thinking of the Teacher of Righteousness? Moreover, a study of the theology of suffering as it appears in the *Hymns* and the other Qumran writings shows that the suffering of the righteous was never presented as an expiation for their sins nor for the redemption of sinners, which is precisely the essential theological contribution of the Servant poems.[22] So once more the resemblance found by Dupont-Sommer between the Teacher of Righteousness and the Man of Sorrows seems to be only a figment of the imagination.

In short, none of the allegations of Dupont-Sommer or of Allegro rest on any texts known at the present time.

And what if future discoveries should produce them? Then Christians would find no difficulty in admitting this historic fact and recognizing that the men of Qumran could have *identified* their venerated Teacher of Righteousness as the Messiah.

But so long as such texts are lacking it is wiser to reserve judgment. This reserve is even more important since there is, for the contrary meaning, a text which seems to exclude this messiahship. The author of the *Hymns*, who ac-

[19] See "Les citations de l'Ancien Testament, et spécialement des Poèmes du Serviteur, dans les Hymnes de Qumrân" in *Revue de Qumrân*, vol. 2, no. 3, pp. 357-394.

[20] Revised Standard Version reads "with blackness."

[21] R.S.V. reads "the tongue of those who are taught."

[22] See "La théologie de la souffrance dans les Hymnes de Qumrân" in *Revue de Qumrân*, vol. 3, no. 3 (1961) pp. 365-386.

cording to Dupont-Sommer is the Teacher of Righteousness himself, quotes in column XVI, line 18, the 132d psalm, verse 10,[23] which reads, in the original, "Turn not away the face of Thine anointed" (from the Davidic king). But in the quotation, he avoids the word "anointed" and replaces it by "servant": "Turn not away the face of Thy servant."

This substitution, obviously intentional, would alone be enough to upset the whole argument of Dupont-Sommer and Allegro. Either the word "anointed" always means "Messiah" when it comes from the pen of a Qumran writer, in which case the author of the *Hymns* (the Teacher of Righteousness) himself disavows this title; or else the word "anointed" is not always employed at Qumran with the meaning of "Messiah", in which case the texts advanced by Dupont-Sommer and Allegro have not the import claimed for them.

2. *Divinity*

The Essenes had such great respect for the transcendence of God that they would have repudiated instinctively any deification of a human being, even so august a person as the Teacher of Righteousness. Dupont-Sommer, however, has attributed to them an astounding credo.

We learn further concerning the Founder that to the elect "God made His Holy Spirit known by means of His Anointed

---

[23] This text is repeated in *II Chron.* 2:42, where a certain number of Hebrew manuscripts have the plural, "thine anointed ones," in place of the singular; but the author of the *Hymns* seems uninfluenced by this variant, since he himself employs the singular.

32

One" (*Damascus Document*, II, 12). God, the Anointed (or Christ) of God, the Spirit of God—these are the three great divine entities in the sect of the New Covenant (*Observations sur le Commentaire d'Habacuc découvert près de la Mer Morte*, p. 25).

The Teacher of Righteousness has revealed the Mysteries of God; "God," it is said, "through His Anointed One, has made us to know His Holy Spirit" (*Dam. A.*, II, 12). In this sentence is outlined something like a trinitarian theology: God, the Anointed One of God, the Spirit of God, such are the three great divine entities in the sect of the New Covenant (*The Dead Sea Scrolls; a Preliminary Survey*, p. 65).

Elsewhere he quotes the *Habakkuk Commentary*. Here is his translation:

The explanation of this refers to the Wicked Priest who has persecuted the Teacher of Righteousness in order to swallow him up in the heat of his anger. Thou hast dared to strip him of his clothing;[1] but at the moment of the sacred rest of the Day of Atonement, he appeared to them all resplendent, to swallow them up and to cause them to stumble on the Day of the Fast, which for them is a sabbath rest."

And from this passage he derives the following picture:

Thus it is the Teacher of Righteousness, shining with a divine splendour, who himself chastises the wicked city. The verb used here, hôphîa', "he was resplendent," occurs several times in the Old Testament to describe the appearance of Yahweh himself. Furthermore the Biblical text here commented on contains the words: *So that God may see their feasts*; and this

[1] Later Dupont-Sommer himself preferred a different translation of this phrase: "In his house of exile" (*Vetus Testamentum* No. 2, (1955), p. 126).

text is applied by the commentator to the Teacher: What an extraordinary apotheosis! (*The Dead Sea Scrolls; a Preliminary Survey*, p. 44).[2]

Moreover, Dupont-Sommer is ever ready to employ the adjective "divine" in speaking of the Teacher of Righteousness: "Divine Founder" (*Ibid.*, p. 22, and "Le Commentaire d'Habacuc," *Revue de l'Histoire des Religions*, 137 [April-June, 1950] 162), . . . "Divine Teacher" (*Ibid.*, p. 149 and *The Dead Sea Scrolls; a Preliminary Survey*, p. 44), . . . not to mention "divine nature" and "divine being," already cited in connection with the "Incarnation" of the Teacher of Righteousness.

Professor Étiemble follows his leader with the same affirmations:

Finally, we know from the *Habakkuk Commentary* and the *Damascus Document* that this Teacher of Righteousness, who was put to death between 67 and 63, was in the real sense a Messiah, an Anointed One, a Christ. About him, in his honor, there sprang up and developed a strictly trinitarian theology —A God, a Holy Spirit, and an Anointed of God who is at the same time the Redeemer of mankind and the Judge of the Nations (*Temps Modernes*, January, 1951, pp. 1290-91).

Now let us examine closely the two passages in the *Habakkuk Commentary* and the *Damascus Document* in which Dupont-Sommer has found a belief in the divinity of the Teacher of Righteousness.[3]

[2] The same interpretation is given in his *Observations sur le Commentaire d'Habacuc découvert près de la Mer Morte*, p. 22.

[3] This has nothing to do with the quite different problem of the divinity of the Messiah, since the Teacher of Righteousness is never presented as the Messiah. Furthermore, even in their thinking about the Messiah (or Messiahs) the men of Qumran seem never to have gone beyond the Jewish idea of the "one sent from God."

Habakkuk Commentary

"He appeared to them, all resplendent"[4] (*Habakkuk Commentary*, XI, 7, translation of Dupont-Sommer).

As almost everybody else agrees, (even Allegro: *The Dead Sea Scrolls*, p. 100), the subject of the verb "to appear" is not the Teacher of Righteousness but rather the Wicked Priest, who tried to catch the Teacher and his disciples unawares as they celebrated, according to their conflicting calendar, the feast of the Day of Atonement. In fact, the Hebrew text is perfectly clear: "This applies to the Wicked Priest, who persecuted the Teacher of Righteousness in order to swallow him up in the heat of his anger, in the house of his exile; and, at the time of the feast of rest on the Day of Atonement, he appeared to them to swallow them up and cause them to fall on the day of the fast of their sabbath of rest." Consequently, Dupont-Sommer's whole argument collapses, since it concerns not the Teacher of Righteousness but the Wicked Priest.

But even supposing that the passage actually referred to the Teacher, would we have the right to talk about "apotheosis" and to suggest that the commentator is more or less identifying the Teacher with Yahweh Himself?

Dupont-Sommer relies on the Hebrew word hôphîa', "he appeared," to prove an allusion to the theophanies of the Old Testament (*Deut.* 33:2; *Pss.* 50:2; 80:2; 94:1).[5] To get a clear idea of the use of these terms at Qumran, let us

[4] This is really a paraphrase, since nothing in the Hebrew text corresponds to "all resplendent."

[5] The same argument is set forth in the *Revue de l'Histoire des Religions*, 137 (April–June, 1950); in *Vetus Testamentum*, No. 3 (1951), p. 212; and in *The Jewish Sect of Qumran and the Essenes*, p. 35.

quote *all* the other texts actually known in which this verb occurs.

Rule of the Community:

"When the lights appear" (the reference here is to the rising of the stars).

War Scroll:

"Appear with glad cries, oh Jerusalem" (XII, 13).
"The day has appeared for us" (XVIII, 10-11).

Hymns:

As sure as the dawn,[6] thou (= God) hast appeared to me at daybr[ea]k (IV, 6).

Thou (= God) hast appeared to me in thy strength at daybreak. (IV, 23)

Their nature became apparent to me in bitterness (V, 31-32).

For Belial[7] partakes in the manifestation of their nature of evil (VII, 3). (Here we have reference to the hosts of evil.)

Thou hast succoured my soul; thou hast exalted my horns ever higher and higher, and I appeared in the sevenfold l[ight] (VII, 23-24).[8]

In thy glory has my light appeared (IX, 26).

From my youth upward hast thou (= God) appeared to me in the wisdom of thy judgment (IX, 31).

Thy truth shall appear as an everlasting glory (XI, 26).

Thy marvelous [   ] to make appear before mine eyes all the hearers of [   ] (XVIII, 6-7).

Damascus Document:

When his deeds shall become apparent, he shall be sent out from the congregation (XX, 3). (Here we have to do with a refractory member.)

When his deeds shall become apparent, let no one condone

---

[6] Reference to *Hos.* 6:3.
[7] Chief of demons, according to Qumran terminology.
[8] Reference to *Isaiah*, 30:26.

with him (XX, 6-7). (This again concerns a refractory member.)

When the glory of God shall appear unto Israel (XX, 25-26).

Two other cases, *The War Scroll*, I;16, and the Collection of *Hymns*, XIV;4, cannot assist us because of serious omissions in the context.

Of these fifteen cases of the use of the verb hôphîa', it is clear that only five refer to God, to His glory or to His truth.[9] Elsewhere they apply to the psalmist, to his light, to his hearers, to Jerusalem, to the day, to the stars, to the works of the guilty (twice), and to the nature of evil beings (twice).

Such figures are decisive. The Hebrew term cannot, *by itself*, prove that "the Teacher's . . . followers considered that God had granted him an exceptional exaltation and a celestial after-life" (*Jewish Sect of Qumran*, p. 32). Nor does anything in the context make the slightest allusion to this altogether extraordinary eventuality.

In short, this passage, which does not refer to the Teacher of Righteousness, and which mentions no supernatural "apparition," simply cannot be advanced as a proof of an "apotheosis" or of any deification whatever.[10]

DAMASCUS DOCUMENT

God, through his anointed one, has made us to know His holy Spirit (*Damascus Document*, II, 12. Translation of Dupont-Sommer).

[9] And again, this is no question of apparitions properly so-called, but only of normal manifestations.

[10] These arguments seem to have convinced Dupont-Sommer, for more recently, in *Les écrits esséniens découverts près de la Mer Morte*, he abandons "all resplendent" and himself translates, "he appeared to them to swallow them up"; and then he specifies in a note that there is "no question, properly speaking, of a supernatural apparition."

This text is part of a preliminary exhortation on the great lessons of sacred history (II, 2–III, 12). In the first section (II, 2, 16) the author considers God's way with His world. In the second part (II, 16–III, 1) he speaks of the deluge and of Noah; in III, 2-4, he treats of Abraham, Isaac and Jacob; in III, 4-9, he alludes to the Exodus, then, in III, 9-12, to the disasters of the period of the Kings. There is thus no question in all of this either of the Teacher of Righteousness or of his congregation.

The general sense shows clearly that, on the contrary, the reference is to the prophets. Accordingly, Yigael Yadin has proposed another reading of the text which ought to win all votes: "He (God) taught them (of old time) through the intermediary of the anointed ones of his spirit of holiness and of the seers of truth" (*Israel Exploration Journal*, No. 3, 1956, pp. 158-59. See also p. 104). Almost at the same time that Yadin made this suggestion, Dupont-Sommer proposed another, (*Evidences*, No. 59 [August-September, 1956], p. 18 and note 19), which amounts almost to the same thing: "He made them to know His holy Spirit through the intermediary of His anointed ones"; and a note specifies: "The 'Anointed ones' are here the prophets who, in the course of the ages, have transmitted the divine revelations to the elect. . . . It could also be translated 'and He taught them through the intermediary of the Anointed ones of His holy Spirit.' "

These explanations give us to understand that Dupont-Sommer would not be likely to write today the sentence about "the three great divine entities," (*Observations sur le Commentaire d'Habacuc,* presented at the Académie des Inscriptions et Belles-Lettres on May 26, 1950), since he has very frankly given up the attempt to find in this passage of the *Damascus Document* the Teacher of Righteousness in the role of Messiah.

Nevertheless, he continues to use the expression "holy Spirit," and to provide it with a capital letter as if the men of Qumran had known the third person of the Holy Trinity. Even though he no longer insists on the second of these "three great divine entities," he seems still to maintain his opinion about the third.

Granted, the Hebrew expression RWH QWDŠ can grammatically be translated by "holy Spirit" or even by "Holy Spirit." But it can just as easily mean merely "spirit of holiness" and refer to the sanctifying influence of God as it appears in the Old Testament (*Isa.* 63:10-11; *Ps.* 51:13; and see also *Wisd.* 1:5 and 9:17).

The best way to settle this question is to consult *all* the texts actually known, to see if one or another makes of this "spirit of holiness" a divine person, or at least a divine entity, like that known to Christian theology. Here are the pertinent passages:

Rule of the Community:

In the spirit of the counsel of the truth of God the ways of man shall be cleansed from all his iniquities[11] so that the light of life may be seen; in the holy spirit[12] in union with his truth he shall be purified of all his iniquities; in the spirit of righteousness and of humility his sin shall be redeemed (III, 6-8).

Then shall God in his truth purge all the works of man; and he shall refine through it the body of man,[13] in order to wipe out every spirit of injustice from the entrails of his body and to purify him in the spirit of holiness from all acts of wickedness (IV, 20-21).

[11] Or else, as Dupont-Sommer translates it, "through the spirit of true counsel with regard to the ways of man, all his iniquities shall be redeemed."

[12] Here the author replaces the noun "holiness" by the adjective "holy." The meaning remains the same.

[13] See Yigael Yadin, "A note on DSD IV, 20," (*Journal of Biblical Literature*, No. 1, [1955], pp. 40–43).

To act according to that which was revealed time and again, and according to what the prophets revealed in his spirit of holiness (VII, 15-16).

When that shall come to pass in Israel, according to all the rules for the establishment by a spirit of holiness of the eternal truth, to expiate the culpability of the offense and the perversity of the sin (IX, 3-4).[14]

Hymns:

I praise thee, Oh Lord, for thou has sustained me with thy strength, and thou hast poured forth upon me thy spirit of holiness (VIII, 6-7).

And tho[u, O G]od, hast placed a barrier around his fruit in the hiding of heroes of might and spirits of holiness, and the flame of the ever-turning fire will not [   ][15] (VIII, 11-12).

From my youth up thou hast appeared to me in the wisdom of thy judgment; in truth thou hast firmly sustained me, and in thy spirit of holiness thou has delighted me (IX, 31-32).

I have known thee, my God, through the spirit thou hast placed in me, and faithfully have I obeyed thy marvellous counsel in thy spirit of holiness; thou hast opened up in the midst of me (the source of) knowledge in the secret of thy wisdom (XII, 11-13).

[spirit (?)] of holiness from olden time [   ] (XIII, 1).

By thy will [have I] come [   ] to thy s[pir]it of holiness, and thus thou makest me move towards thine understanding (XIV, 13).

[   ] in the spirit of holi[ness] (XVI, 2).

[   ] spirit of holine[ss] (XVI, 3).

[   ] and to be strengthened in [thy] spirit of hol[iness] (XVI, 7).

To purify me in thy spirit of holiness and to go forward in thy

[14] See *Revue Biblique*, No. 4 [1956], pp. 524–32.

[15] The author is paraphrasing the expulsion from Eden (*Gen.* 3:24). The "heroes of might and spirits of holiness" here take the place of the cherubim.

loving-kindness, "according to the greatness of thy favor"[16] (XVI, 12).

[   ] thou hast poured forth [thy] spirit of holiness upon thy servant (XVII, 26).

Damascus Document:

He (God) taught them (of olden time) through the agency of his anointed ones of his spirit of holiness and of the seers of the truth (II, 12-13).[17]

They have sullied even their spirit of holiness [sic] (V, 11).

Man shall not pollute his spirit of holiness [sic] (VII, 4).

Collection of Benedictions:

May he (God) reward thee (the high priest) with the spirit of holiness and of gra[ce] (*Qumran Cave I*, No. 28 b, pp. 118-30).

Collection of Liturgical Prayers:

Thou hast renewed thy covenant for them in a vision of glory, and the words of thy [spirit] of holiness in the works of thy hands (*Qumran Cave I*, No. 34 bis, p. 154).

Unknown Work:

[   ] the [   ] in thy spirit of holiness (*Qumran Cave I*, No. 39, p. 143).

After having thus reviewed *all* the texts hitherto known concerning the "spirit of holiness," we can assert with confidence the following facts:

1. In the plural the "spirits of holiness" are equated with the angels (*Hymns*, VIII, 12).

2. In the singular the "spirit of holiness" is never presented as a person and is never even the subject of a sentence.

3. This "spirit of holiness" is placed on a par with the

[16] Quotation from *Baruch* 2:27.
[17] This text has already been cited on p. 21.

other "qualities" of God—strength, grace, right, truth, wisdom, intelligence.

4. This "spirit of holiness" is set in opposition to the spirit of iniquity (*Rule of the Community*, IV, 20-21).

5. This "spirit of holiness" can be sullied by the malice of man (*Damascus Document*, V, 11 and VII, 4).

These facts positively exclude any identification of the "spirit of holiness" of Qumran and the "Holy Spirit" of the Christian revelation. On the contrary, they establish in a decisive fashion that for the men of Qumran the "spirit of holiness" meant the sanctifying influence of God, which works in souls to produce holiness, just as it also produces in them strength, wisdom and intelligence. Moreover, this same Jewish and Qumranian conception of "the spirit of holiness" is also to be found in the New Testament, much of which stands at the Jewish level of thinking on this point, as, for example, *Matthew* 12:32, *Mark* 3:29, 12:36, 13:10, *Luke* 10:21, etc. If we reread the Qumran texts, replacing "spirit of holiness" by "sanctifying influence," we can then see the complete equivalence of these two expressions.

But if this is so, the third of these "three great divine entities" evaporates just like the second.

The Essenes were so ardently monotheistic and so passionately convinced of the divine transcendence that they adored God without any knowledge of the mystery of the Holy Trinity; and they adored only God, without any assimilation to Himself of any creature, even their Teacher of Righteousness.

Quite otherwise than Dupont-Sommer, who sees in the Qumran texts a Christian concept of the Holy Spirit, Charles F. Potter is unable to find the Holy Ghost of Christian theology either in the Essene writings or in the New Testament. According to him,

When the Qumran manuscripts are properly recognized and evaluated in relation to the books in our very much edited and expurgated New Testament, the doctrine of the Holy Spirit will have to go, and will take with it the doctrine of the Trinity, which never was in the New Testament anyway (*The Lost Years of Jesus Revealed*, p. 103).

It is true that, so far as the Essenes are concerned, Potter's conclusions are in entire accord with the texts we have just been considering.

At times one gets the impression that the Holy Spirit is synonymous with Truth or Righteousness or Justice, and that the Essenes were struggling hard to express and emphasize the importance of this abstract idea without personifying it enough to make it a rival of God (*Ibid.*, p. 106).

On the other hand, the Holy Spirit, third person of the Holy Trinity, is so clearly revealed in the New Testament that it is hard to see how Potter could evade the testimony of these explicit passages:

Make disciples of all nations, baptising them in the name of the Father and of the Son and of the Holy Spirit (*Matt.* 28:19, confirmed by the *Acts of the Apostles*, 2:38, 10:48, 19:2-3).
But the Counselor, the Holy Spirit, whom the Father will send in my name, he will teach you all things (*John* 14:26).
When the Counselor comes, whom I shall send to you from the Father, he will bear witness to me (*John* 15:26).
[Jesus] being therefore exalted at the right hand of God, and having received from the Father the promise of the Holy Spirit, he has poured out this Spirit . . . (*Acts* 2:33).
The grace of the Lord Jesus Christ and the love of God, and the fellowship of the Holy Spirit be with you all . . . (*II Cor.* 13:14).
God has sent the Spirit of His Son into our hearts, crying, "Abba, Father" (*Gal.* 4:6).

We can surely recognize easily enough the weakness of the fundamental postulate that vitiates all Potter's work. Since he assumes (without proving it)that primitive Christianity was hardly distinguishable from Essenism, and since he finds no Holy Spirit among the Essenes, he concludes therefore that the Holy Spirit must have been unknown to Jesus and His disciples also. If he wishes to reason fairly he ought to say just the opposite: that since the doctrine of the Holy Spirit does exist in the New Testament, but is not found among the texts at Qumran, this is a proof that Christianity is completely different from Essenism. But in that case he would have to renounce his thesis and recognize that his theories are from the realm of fantasy and not from the domain of scholarship.

As for Dupont-Sommer, he has yet another argument to try out. The veneration accorded the Teacher of Righteousness is more or less similar to the immense respect in which the Essenes held the Divine Majesty. Like all Jews, the Essenes avoided pronouncing the name of Yahweh, too sacred to be uttered by human lips. Also, they never used the name of the Teacher of Righteousness. Therefore, the Teacher of Righteousness must have shared in the transcendence of God.

The founder (in the Habakkuk Commentary) is never referred to by his name; he is generally called the "Teacher of Righteousness," *moré hassèdhèk*. Twice he is called the "Elect of God, *Behír El*. If he is thus anonymous, it is not only because of the mysterious style of the author, but over and above all because of the intense veneration of which the person of the Teacher had become the object. His name was unpronounceable like the very name of Yahweh (*Observations sur le Commentaire d'Habacuc*, p. 14).

In *The Dead Sea Scrolls; a Preliminary Survey* (p. 33)

he redevelops the same argument, but with the omission of an essential phrase:

The sect had as its founder a person who is generally called the Teacher of Righteousness (Moré hassèdhèk); twice he is given the title of "Elect of God" (Behír El). Never is he called by his own name. If he is thus anonymous, it is because of the intense veneration of which the person of the Teacher had become the object; his name was unpronounceable, like the name of Yahweh.

Elsewhere, Dupont-Sommer gives a fuller explanation:

Object of an intense religious veneration, his name was unpronounceable, like the very name of Yahweh. This is why he remains for us the Anonymous One. Let us remember that according to the testimony of Josephus, "the name of the Lawgiver was, after God, a great object of veneration" . . . and that "whoever should blaspheme against it was punished by death" (*B.J.*, II, S, 9, 145; cf. II, 8, 10, 152). The "Lawgiver" here is not Moses; Josephus always mentions Moses by his name. It is, according to me, precisely our Teacher of Righteousness.[18]

When we look more closely at this argument, we see that it is open to a number of objections. In the first place, Josephus never speaks of the "founder" of Essenism,[19] nor of the Teacher of Righteousness. It is therefore unreasonable to suppose that he would, without further

---

[18] *Revue de l'Histoire des Religions*, 137 (April-June, 1950), 153. A later exposition of the same theories appeared in *Evidences*, No. 55, March, [1956], p. 30, note 18.

[19] To go back to the term used by Dupont-Sommer. But the *Damascus Document* (I, 10–11) suggests that the "sect" was founded about twenty years before the Teacher of Righteousness became a member.

explanation, refer to him under the ambiguous term of "Lawgiver."

Next, Josephus uses this particular term, "law-giver" in reference to Moses: "The wise institutions of their law-giver, Moses" . . . "Moses, the law-giver of the Jews" . . . "Moses, their law-giver" (*Antiquities of the Jews*,[20] Pro-emium 4:18; III:6, 95; I, XV, 1, 240).

Again, Josephus does not say that the name of this personage was unpronounceable, but only that is was, "after God, a great object of veneration," and that those who blasphemed it should be punished by death.

Furthermore, nothing indicates that, even among the Essenes, the name of the Teacher of Righteousness was unpronounceable. The documents actually known do not mention him; this is a fact. But "unpronounced" and "unpronounceable" are not synonymous.

Finally, the Teacher of Righteousness was not the only victim of this mania for anonymity. The "Wicked Priest," the "Lion of Wrath," the "Man of the Lie," the "Builders of the Walls," the "Seekers of Moderation"—all these remain for us mysterious unknowns. Must we then believe

---

[20] This is also the usage of Philo, as Dupont-Sommer himself recognizes in *Evidences* No. 54, January, 1956, p. 24, note 10. Moreover, here is what Goosens, who is generally very favorable to Dupont-Sommer, thinks on this point: "I can find only one real objection to make to Dupont-Sommer. . . . He sees here an allusion to the law-giver of the sect, that is to say to the Teacher of Righteousness. . . . I am forced to refuse any weight to this argument, for I have counted a dozen passages in the *Contra Apion* where Moses is referred to by the title of Law-giver" (*La Nouvelle Clio*, No. 10, [1950], p. 645, note 26).

Quite recently M. Philonenko has called attention to the importance of the "additions" to the text of Josephus contained in the Slavic version ("La notice du Joseph Slave sur les Esséniens," in *Semitica*, VI, 69–73). Now this Slavic version in one place substitutes *their* law-giver for *the* law-giver (II, VIII, 10, 152), and then this wording could refer to the law-giver of the Essenes, the

that the names of all these persons were equally unpronounceable "like the very name of Yahweh"?

In fact, if the various Essene writers do not give us the
real name of the Teacher of Righteousness, the reason is
certainly the one which Dupont-Sommer mentioned in the
Observations sur le Commentaire d'Habacuc, but which he
omitted in *The Dead Sea Scrolls; a Preliminary Survey:*
"It is . . . because of the mysterious style of the author."
The men of Qumran habitually substituted for proper
names—which seemed too banal for their taste—allegorical
titles which expressed either filial homage or clever carica-
ture. With time these circumlocutions have obviously
become extremely mysterious for us. But this custom, so
regrettable for historians, has nothing to do with the
religious practice, observed by all Jews, of surrounding the
proper name of God, Yahweh, with a respect so deep that
they refrained even from pronouncing it. The Teacher of
Righteousness was a piously venerated personage, yes; but
he was not on this evidence alone a superhuman being
more or less assimilated into the Majesty of God.

Teacher of Righteousness, as well as to the law-giver of the Jews,
Moses. But in paragraph 145, just where Josephus says that "after
the name of God, that of the law-giver is the object of profound
veneration for them," the Slavic version also uses *"the* law-giver"
and not *"their* law-giver." It is only in paragraph 152, where he
is dealing with the tortures inflicted by the Romans on the Essenes
to make them apostasize, that the Slavic version uses *"their* law-
giver." Therefore, we should attribute this variation to the whim
of the translator rather than to the trustworthiness of his basic
document. Philonenko's reasoning could be valid for the Slavic
"addition" (which are really Greek omissions), in so far as it deals
with entire phrases or parts of sentences; but it can hardly be used
as proof in each of the little details by which every translator introduces more or less of his own personal interpretation. Moreover,
the accuracy of the Russian translator is strongly attacked in the
recent study by Mescerskij (reviewed by S. Szyszman in *Revue de
Qumran,* No. 3 [Feb. 1959], pp. 451–58).

3. Passion and Crucifixion

The *Habakkuk Commentary* and the other parallel "commentaries" frequently mention a conflict between the Teacher of Righteousness and the Wicked Priest. The latter persecuted his adversary, inflicted acts of violence upon him, obliged him to flee into exile, and even tried, subsequently, to capture him. But can we go on to deduce from this a "Passion" and a "Crucifixion" of the Teacher of Righteousness? Dupont-Sommer thinks so.

The similarities, appearing in every aspect between the Jewish New Covenant, sealed in the blood of the Teacher of Righteousness in 63 B.C. and the Christian New Covenant, sealed in the blood of the Galilean Teacher about 30 A.D. . . . (*Observations sur le Commentaire d'Habacuc*, p. 29).

We can understand from this that the Teacher was crucified. Elsewhere we learn further that he was "stripped of his garments," doubtless to be scourged and hung on the cross (*Revue de l'Histoire des Religions*, 137 [April–June, 1950], pp. 147 and 164).

From all the evidence this passage alludes to the Passion of the Teacher of Righteousness; he was judged, condemned, tortured (*The Dead Sea Scrolls; a Preliminary Survey*, p. 34).

In the fever of these days, Aristobulus . . . could quite well decide to end this dangerous opposition by condemning its leader, and perhaps also some of his principal supporters, and having them summarily executed (*The Dead Sea Scrolls; a Preliminary Survey*, p. 36).

A whole article in *Vetus Testamentum* (No. 3, [1951], pp. 200-15) is devoted to attempting to prove that "the Teacher of Righteousness was actually put to death" (p. 215 ff).

Later Dupont-Sommer very properly abandoned his translation "thou hast dared to strip him of his clothing" for "in his house of exile" and thus lost his allusions to scourging and crucifixion; but he maintains his other points of view. As he writes,

(This) partial correction . . . changes no essential of our earlier exegesis of the whole of the sentence. It even confirms, we think, the thesis we have always maintained—the assurance that the Teacher of Righteousness was actually put to death (*The Dead Sea Scrolls; a Preliminary Survey*, p. 36).
This august Teacher was made to suffer, was put to death (*Vetus Testamentum*, No. 2, (1955) p. 126).

Even more than Dupont-Sommer, Allegro is committed to this view. Let us recall the passage from *Time* magazine already cited on page 10:

The mysterious "Teacher of Righteousness," whom he [Alexander Jannaeus] turned over to his mercenaries to be crucified . . .
. . . When the Jewish king had left (the community) took down the broken body of their Master to stand guard over it until Judgment Day (*Ibid.*).

By way of pointing up these opinions Allegro gives us in his book, *The Dead Sea Scrolls*, an exciting account of the moment of conflict, worthy of the pen of an eyewitness:

This practice of crucifying his political enemies is credited to the Lion of Wrath in the *Nahum Commentary*, and it further comments that this was never before done in Israel, being essentially a foreign punishment. One might surmise that the Sectarians had particular cause to recall this activity of Jannaeus, since their Master had suffered the same cruel death, the recognized punishment of a rebel.
    The *Habakkuk Commentary* makes a point of its being the Day of Atonement when the Wicked Priest confronted the

Master and his followers in the "house of their exile." This might imply, if what I have said about the temporary sanctuary at Qumran is correct, that the Master was even then officiating at the altar when Jannaeus appeared. In any case, the scene as these two priests faced one another must have been dramatic enough. The one, haughty and proud, scarred by the wounds of many battles, and the ravaging of a lifetime of greed and lechery, the other, white-robed and saintly, gazing scornfully on his enemy, secure in his simple trust in God and the hope of resurrection to eternal life. Would that those disciples, who perhaps watched the scene from the crags above the Monastery, had included a Mark or a Luke. But connected narratives of this type have no place in Qumran literature (p. 100).

To be sure, Jesus is not the only innocent man in history who was put to death, even by crucifixion. The Christian faith would be in no way compromised if the Teacher of Righteousness had also, in his turn, ended his life in martyrdom. For it is essentially by virtue of His divine personality that the death of Jesus has redemptive value. Yet in order to make Jesus and the Teacher comparable, it must first be proved that the Teacher was actually crucified and put to death.

What we should do then is to consult the texts alleged to refer to this death by crucifixion since, in the prudent words of Dupont-Sommer, "Only the texts can decide" (*Vetus Testamentum*, No. 3, 1951, p. 200).

Habakkuk Commentary

The explanation of this refers to the House of Absalom and its supporters, who were silent when the Teacher of Righteousness was punished and did not aid him against the Man of Untruth who had scorned the Law in the midst of all the peoples (V, 9-12).

. . . struck by him in the execution of iniquitous judgments;

and odious profaners committed horrors on him, and vengeance on his body of flesh . . . (IX, 1-2).

The explanation of this refers to the Wicked Priest, whom,
through sin committed against the Teacher of Righteousness
and his supporters, God has delivered into the hands of his
enemies to humiliate him by beating him to death, in bitterness of soul, because he had committed a crime against his
Elect (IX, 9-12).[1]

This applies to the Wicked Priest, who persecuted the Teacher
of Righteousness, to swallow him up in the heat of his anger,
in the house of his exile, and, at the time of the festival of
rest of the Day of Atonement, he appeared to them to swallow
them up and to make them fall, on the day of fasting of their
Sabbath of rest (XI, 4-8).[2]

Nahum Commentary

. . . Its interpretation concerns the Lion of Wrath[3] . . .
death (?) Seekers after compromise used to hang (or hangs)
men up alive . . . which was never done (?) before in Israel,
for it (the Scripture)[4] calls the one hanged alive on the tree
. . .[5]

Damascus Document

From the day of the gathering in of the Teacher of the Community . . . (XIX, 35-XX, 1).

From the day of the gathering in of the Instructor of the Community . . . (XX, 14).

These are all the texts that are actually known. How
should they be interpreted?

[1] These three translations are by Dupont-Sommer.

[2] Translation by Carmignac. See pp. 33-37 for several grave
objections to the translation of Dupont-Sommer.

[3] Perhaps identical with the Wicked Priest, as Allegro also thinks.

[4] A better reading of this passage would be: "For it is written
concerning one who is hanged alive on a tree." The author is here
referring to Deut. 21:22-23.

[5] Text as edited and restored by Allegro in Journal of Biblical
Literature, No. 2 [1956], pp. 89-95.

In the first place it is certain that the Teacher of Righteousness was sentenced and subjected to horrible treatment; but the text tells us no more about it, and we have no right to invent anything. Elsewhere there are allusions to persecution and even to exile. The Wicked Priest went so far as to exploit the Day of Atonement, which was kept as a solemn Sabbath, to attempt to lay hands on his adversary.[6] All this the texts state clearly. But they never speak of the martyrdom of the Teacher of Righteousness. They reproach the Wicked Priest indignantly for having "appeared" in order to "swallow up" his victim; but they are silent as to any actual capture or real "engorgement." The commentator stigmatizes the Lion of Wrath, who was accustomed to "hang living men" (crucifixion?). But he does not accuse him of having applied this torture to his beloved Teacher. Can we argue from the omissions in our texts, and suppose that by accident all the passages that mention the bloody death of the Teacher of Righteousness have been destroyed? That would be possible; but in that case we should present this martyrdom and this crucifixion as pure hypotheses and not as historical certainties!

In his most recent book (*The Treasure of the Copper Scroll*, 1960, p. 72) Allegro introduces a new suggestion. One of the scrolls, he claims,

. . . tells us cryptically, by an ingenious word play, how, on a certain Day of Atonement, the Wicked Priest appeared at the Teacher's "house of exile" and "made him swallow the cup of his poison," a well-understood euphemism for "put him to death." The manner of his death can hardly be doubted, since there were no circumstances that should make it differ from that meted out to the 800 other rebels. Furthermore, one cannot help suspecting that Jesus's frequent use of the same

---

[6] This stratagem was made possible by the difference between the calendar of the Essenes and the official calendar.

phrase about "the cup," when he too is going to his crucifixion at the instigation of a Jewish High Priest, is more than coincidental (cf. *Mt.* 20:22-23; 26:39; *Jn.* 18:11, etc.).

It is to be regretted that Allegro has not identified the passage in question, which has a ring of familiarity in spite of a startling note of difference. Unfortunately for his argument, the Hebrew verb *bâla'* always means "devour" or "swallow up" as in the following passages: (*Gen.* 41:7, 24) "And the thin ears swallowed up the seven plump and full ears"; (*Exod.* 15:12) "The earth swallowed them"; (*Num.* 16:32) "And the earth opened its mouth and swallowed them up"; (*Job* 7:19) "Nor let me alone till I swallow my spittle?" (*Ps.* 69:15) "Let not the flood sweep over me, or the deep swallow me up, or the pit close its mouth over me," etc. Consequently, even if this verb had the word "cup" as its object it would not mean "drink the contents of the cup," but rather "swallow the cup itself," "devour the metal."

But this is not all. In the *Habakkuk Commentary*, XI: 14-15, the only passage in the Dead Sea Scrolls which joins the terms "swallow up" and "cup," the cup is not the object of the verb but is itself the subject: "The cup of the wrath of [G]od will devour him"—even as in the text of *Habakkuk* which is the subject of the comment: "The cup in the Lord's right hand—will come around to you and shame will come upon your glory" (2:16).

To affirm, therefore, that such an expression could have been a source of the Gospel formularies, "drink of the cup," of *Mt.* 20:22, 23; 26:39, 42; (and *Mk.* 10:38-39, 14: 36; *Lk.* 22:42; *Jn.* 18:11) is to go far beyond the evidence of the text.

Moreover, even considered as a simple hypothesis, this imaginary crucifixion is contradicted by the double testimony of the *Damascus Document*, in which the author speaks explicitly of the death of the Teacher of Righteousness. How does he describe it? As execution? martyrdom? assassination? Not at all. He uses instinctively a term filled with serenity, the passive of the verb, *asaf*, to reunite. The death of the Teacher of Righteousness was for him "being gathered" to his fathers. Now this is precisely the term used in the Bible for the passing of the patriarchs: Abraham (*Gen.*, 25:8), Isaac (*Gen.*, 35:29), Aaron (*Num.*, 20:24), and Moses (*Deut.*, 32:50). This similarity, which must be more than coincidence, is enough to prove to us that for the men of Qumran the death of the Teacher of Righteousness called up no memory of a dramatic slaughter, but only a gathering up into the sleep of the just, in the peace of the Lord.

This examination of the texts explains the formal denial brought against Allegro by the other scholars who were charged, like himself, with editing the Qumran manuscripts. Thus, in the (London) *Times,*

We find [in the texts] no crucifixion of the "teacher," no deposition from the cross, and no "broken body of their Master" to be stood guard over until Judgment Day. . . . It is our conviction that either he has misread the texts or he has built up a chain of conjecture which the materials do not support (March 16, 1956, p. 11).

And we can understand the embarrassment Allegro must have felt in trying to justify his first statements:

Any such reconstruction must of necessity be based largely on inference, since nothing in the nature of a history book or "Gospel" of the New Testament type has been or is likely to be forthcoming from Qumran. We shall not, therefore, expect to find Hebrew texts giving intimate details of the lives of Qumran personalities. We do have certain vague references in Biblical commentaries from the sect's library which have to be interpreted as best we can.

We know, for instance, that the teacher was persecuted by a certain "wicked priest" in the "house of his exile," presumed to be Qumran. It was long ago suggested that this persecutor could be identified with Alexander Jannaeus, the Jewish priest-king of the second and first centuries B.C., and this view has steadily gained ground among scholars. From Josephus we learn that Jannaeus practised the cruel punishment of crucifixion, and, indeed, on one occasion had 800 Pharisaic rebels executed in this way in Jerusalem, following an unsuccessful revolt. From this alone it would have been a not unreasonable inference that the teacher suffered the same fate, since he, too, had rebelled against the Jerusalem priesthood. But now, as my colleagues are well aware, a newly discovered Biblical commentary from Qumran not only offers some support for the Jannaeus dating by certain historical allusions, but mentions this practice of crucifixion, or, as it says, "hanging men up alive."

Since the commentator of Qumran does not refer to events unless they have a special importance for himself or his time, we can reasonably suppose that this form of execution had had some connection with their own history, even though the commentary nowhere mentions their Master. . . .

Nevertheless, important as this allusion is, the theory remains only an inference, claiming only probability, and I have myself never gone further than this in advancing it (The Times, [London] March 20, 1956, p. 13).

Thus Allegro himself recognizes that the "crucifixion" of the Teacher of Righteousness is not mentioned in the documents, that it is purely personal "reconstruction," that it is based only on a "certain vague allusion," and that even the passage in question[7] nowhere mentions the Teacher of Righteousness.

It may be conceded, if that were his purpose, that his deductions would not be "unreasonable" in the construc-

[7] *Nahum Commentary*, 1, 6–8, cited above, p. 51.

tion of a historical novel. But they remain without value for a historian who is faithful to the texts and who has the double witness of the *Damascus Document*.

4. *Resurrection and Second Coming*

If we insist upon seeing the life of the Teacher of Righteousness as in every detail the model for that of Jesus, obviously we must have a "Resurrection" after the "Passion" and "Crucifixion."

In order to prepare the ground for this scene, in presenting his "findings" over BBC television, Allegro declared that the disciples of the Teacher "took down the broken body of their Master to stand guard over it until Judgment Day. For they believed . . . their Master would rise again" (*Time*, February 6, 1956, p. 88).

A little later he tried to justify this "reconstruction" by various arguments whose value must be judged by the reader.

Years ago it was suggested by scholars that the teacher was expected to rise again as priestly Messiah. Allusions gleaned from a number of unpublished fragments from the caves seem to support this idea, and an article now in preparation will lay most of the new messianic material before scholars in the next few months. But it must be appreciated again that we have no detailed theological treatise from Qumran, comparable, for instance, with the Pauline letters, and we can only work by inference. Yet, if indeed the Covenanters did expect the resurrection of their teacher, as I am convinced they did, then they must have buried him with particular care, and, if he had been crucified, taken his body down from the stake, instead of leaving it to moulder there, as was the custom with this form of execution (*The Times*, March 20, 1956, p. 13).

Finally, in his book *The Dead Sea Scrolls*, Allegro sets forth the same opinions again.

> The Qumran sect looked to the coming of a Priestly Messiah, whom they call the "Teacher of Righteousness" and "Interpreter of the Law." The fact that these are precisely the terms they apply to the priestly founder of the Sect supports the idea that it was none other than their resurrected Teacher who would lead the theocratic community of the New Israel in the Last Days. . . . The Covenanters were presumably still waiting for the Resurrection of their Master when they were swept away (*The Dead Sea Scrolls*, pp. 148 and 162).

In short, Allegro does not say that the Teacher of Righteousness actually rose from the dead, but merely ascribes to his followers an unquenchable hope for his resurrection. Yet he brings forth no text in favor of such a faith. He offers us only "allusions gleaned from a number of unpublished fragments from the fourth cave."[1]

Now that he has himself published these new materials[2] we can assess their evidential value. These "allusions gleaned in a number of unpublished fragments" are reduced to a single passage; and it is not even certain that this passage refers to the Teacher of Righteousness, since it is Allegro who has restored it in a lacuna. This passage

---

[1] As the unpublished texts are kept strictly secret, they could be known only by Allegro and his colleagues; and as these co-workers protest specifically against his interpretations, it is hard to see how these could have been the origin of the idea of a "Resurrection," as tentatively put forth by other scholars . . . whose names, moreover, are not mentioned.

[2] "Further Light on the History of the Qumran Sect," *Journal of Biblical Literature*, No. 2, 1956, pp. 89–95; "More *Isaiah* Commentaries from Qumran's Fourth Cave," *Ibid.*, No. 3, 1958, pp. 215–21; "Fragments of a Qumran Scroll of Eschatalogical Midrashim," *Ibid.*, No. 4, 1958, pp. 350–54; "A Recently Discovered Fragment of a Commentary on Hosea from Qumran's Fourth Cave," *Ibid.*, No. 2, 1959, pp. 142–47.

speaks nowhere of resurrection, nor of posthumous influence, nor even of survival close to God.[3] The passage is limited to using a text from Psalm 37: 32-33 which contains the expressions "seeketh to slay him," and "God will not leave him."

Here is the document as it has been published by Allegro and with the restitutions proposed by himself.

The wicked watcheth for the righteous and seeketh [to slay him. The Lord will not leave him in his hand, nor] condemn him when he is judged. Its interpretation concerns the wicked [pries]t who s[ent to the Teacher of Righteousness . . .?] to slay him [. . .] and the Law which he sent to him. But God will not le[ave him in his hand] nor [condemn him when] he is judged. And [God will] repay to [him] his recompense to give him into the hand of terrible ones of the Gentiles to do to him [. . .] (*Journal of Biblical Literature* No. 2, [June, 1956] p. 94).

Merely because Psalm 37 contains the words "God will not abandon him," and because the commentator seems to apply them to the Teacher of Righteousness, we hardly have the right to conclude that the disciples of the Teacher awaited his resurrection.

Far more imposing are the many arguments brought up to prove the "Second Coming," the glorious return of the Teacher of Righteousness at the end of time to judge the world. Time and again Dupont-Sommer affirms this article of the Essene creed as definitely proven:

The Cairo document[4] speaks expressly of "the coming of the Teacher of Righteousness at the end of days" (*Observations on the Habakkuk Commentary*, p. 25).

[3] Nevertheless we know that the Essenes believed in the immortality of souls and in the influence of the dead from beyond the grave.

[4] Usually called the *Damascus Document*.

It is the Elect of God, that is to say the Teacher of Righteousness, who, by delegation from God, will exercise the functions of judge at the Last Judgment (*Revue de l'Histoire des Religions,* 137 [April-June, 1950], 157).

Thus the Final Judgment will be exercised by the Elect of God, that is to say by the Teacher of Righteousness. It will reach all the heathen nations at the same time as Israel . . . Let us stress that at the time of the supreme Visitation the functions of Judge are entrusted by God to the Teacher of Righteousness. . . . Yes, it is necessary to keep watch, for the Master must return "at the end of the days": this belief—which we remember is also that of the author of the *Habakkuk Commentary*—is clearly and frequently stated in the *Damascus Document*. The day of the last Judgment is at hand; life is lived in this expectation which is at once terrible and consoling (*The Dead Sea Scrolls; a Preliminary Survey,* pp. 43 and 64).

"During the time of the wickedness until the coming of the Anointed of Aaron and Israel" (XII, 23), "when the Anointed of Aaron and Israel shall come" (XIX, 10-11), "until the coming of the Anointed (born) from Aaron and Israel" (XX, 1). All these passages refer to the coming of the Anointed at the end of the days, when the period of wickedness will definitely be ended and the last Judgment shall take place. Who is this Anointed? Is he purely a future, transcendent Messiah, the hero of the only world to come? Or has this Anointed a destiny and an earthly career? It would seem that the answer is to be found in another sentence of the same *Damascus Document* (VI, 10-11), "during the whole time of the wickedness until the coming of the Teacher of Righteousness at the end of the days." This text is fundamental (*The Jewish Sect of Qumran and the Essenes,* p. 54).

This august teacher was tormented and put to death, but he lives forever, and his faithful await his return, at the same time as the coming of the Messiah of Israel, the King-Messiah, at the end of time. . . . The mysterious Teacher of Righteousness, this sacerdotal Messiah who was tormented and put to death about one hundred years before Jesus of Nazareth and whose faithful await his glorious return at the end of time (*Evidences*, No. 56, April, 1956, pp. 17 and 25, and *Encyclopédie Française*, 19, 42-44).

In the land of exile, convinced that the Teacher of Righteousness, whom the high priest had put to death, would return at the end of time, the disciples regrouped themselves, reorganized, settled down, awaiting the great Day, the supreme Visit of God (*Evidences*, No. 59, August, 1956, p. 13).

These assertions are accepted without discussion by other authors as well. Thus, for example:

The *Habakkuk Commentary* brings us then "an extraordinary revelation, that of a divine Master, of a Messiah, whose return, a glorious second coming, was awaited with fervour about a century before the appearance of the Galilean Master, the Messiah of the Christian faith" (R. Goosens, "Onaïs le Juste, le Messie de la Nouvelle Alliance, lapidé à Jérusalem en 65 avant J.-C.," *La Nouvelle Clio*, No. 7, p. 340).

(The Teacher of Righteousness) ascended into Heaven, near God, judged and condemned Jerusalem; he will participate, at the end of time, in the Supreme Tribunal. He founded a Church whose faithful await his glorious return (J.-L. Bory, *Express*, Paris, December 7, 1956, p. 22).

In the face of this barrage of statements in favor of a Second Coming of the Teacher of Righteousness, how are we to assess the truth?

The opinion of Dupont-Sommer is based entirely on two texts that he considers decisive. To examine them in turn:

Habakkuk Commentary, V:3-5

Dupont-Sommer gives the following translation, which has been adopted by a number of other authors:

The explanation of this is that God will not destroy His people by means of the nations. But it is by means of His Elect that God will execute judgment on all the nations; and it is at the time of their chastisement that all the sinful from amongst His people will make atonement.

Thus, he concludes,

... the final judgment will be exercised by the Elect of God, that is to say, the Teacher of Righteousness (*The Dead Sea Scrolls; a Preliminary Survey*, p. 43).

There has been a lively discussion over a number of years as to whether the Hebrew word for the "elect"—BHYRW, as it is written here and in IX:12—should not be considered plural rather than singular in meaning, and whether Dupont-Sommer has not misread the text in consequence. But the argument is really without point, for in either case it is obvious that this "elect" is not the Teacher of Righteousness. The author clearly wishes to express his thought by the opposition of symmetrical terms: "God will not destroy His people by the hand of (or by means of, as Dupont-Sommer translates it) the nations, but by the hand of His elect God will execute the judgment of all nations." According to the laws of Semitic parallelism, "His elect" should here be synonymous with "His people."[5]

Thus we must recognize that his "elect" is "the people of God," visibly represented by the Essene community. This idea occurs, moreover, at Qumran. An entire book, the *War Scroll*, describes this destruction of all the nations; and the task is performed neither by the Teacher of Righteousness nor by the Messiah. It is the Children of

[5] This equivalence is also to be seen in *Isaiah* 43:20, "My people, my chosen" and in Ps. 105:43, "his people with joy, his chosen with gladness."

Light, at first almost destroyed by the heathen, who finally succeed in exterminating them:

It will be a time of tribulation [for al]l the people redeemed of God; in all their tribulations there has been none like it from the beginning (?) until the consummation of the eternal redemption (I, 11-12).

Moreover, by the hand of Thine anointed, the man who had vision of things foreordained . . . Thou hast waged battle against our foes and caused the troops of Belial[6]—the seven vain nations[7]—to fall into the hands of the pauper folk whom Thou didst redeem . . . (XI, 8-9).

Into the hands of the needy hast Thou delivered the foeman in all lands, and into the hands of them that were bowed to the dust. So hast Thou humbled the mighty of the peoples; brought their deserts upon the wicked; vindicated among all men the truthfulness of Thy judgments . . . (XI, 13-14).

. . . on earth Thou hast likewise placed at Thy service the elect of an holy people . . . and when Thou contendest in judgment Thou wilt muster an army of [these] Thine elect . . . and they shall prevail in battle and, along with the heavenly elect be trium[phant] (XII, 1 and 5).[8]

Isn't this a more accurate exposition of the thought so briefly outlined in the *Habakkuk Commentary*? But if it is so, we have established that the last judgment of all the nations will be executed by the hand (or by means) of the elect people—not by the hand (or by means) of the Teacher of Righteousness.

Even if we go still further, however, and concede to

[6] The king of demons.
[7] The seven nations dispossessed by the Israelites when they conquered Canaan.
[8] These texts are translated by Gaster, *Dead Sea Scrolls*, pp. 295-96 (Translator's note).

Dupont-Sommer that this "elect" could be a particular person, must we then identify him in this passage with the Teacher of Righteousness? By no means. For an *Isaiah Commentary*[9] actually does attribute the "judgment of all the nations" to a definite individual—but this is the "shoot of David," that is to say, the Messiah of Israel who will restore the Davidic dynasty, and not the Teacher of Righteousness, who was a priest and consequently descended from Aaron.

[The shoot of] David, who arises at the en[d of days] . . . he shall rule over all the [nation]s . . . his sword shall judge [al]l peoples.[10]

Damascus Document, VII, 10-11

For Dupont-Sommer this text is irrefutable proof. He translates it: "Until the coming of the Teacher of Righteousness at the end of the days," and he comments thus:

The Teacher of Righteousness has died, but he will rise from the dead "at the end of the days"—that is to say, at the fulfillment of the time, when "all the time of wickedness" shall have been accomplished. This expectation of the return of the Teacher of Righteousness, set forth here so clearly, is one of the basic doctrines of the creed of the faithful of the New Covenant (*Evidences*, No. 59, [August, 1956], p. 21 and note 71).

The word "Teacher" MWRH, however, does not occur in the Hebrew, which uses YWRH instead. Now this word may derive from the same root and mean "autumn rain,"

[9] Published and restored by Allegro: *Journal of Biblical Literature*, No. 3, 1956, pp. 174-87.
[10] Document III, fragment D, lines 1, 4, 5. It should be observed that this text could not have been known to Dupont-Sommer at the time when he was studying the *Habakkuk Commentary*, and that otherwise his interpretation would doubtless have been different.

or "he who brings rain," as it is also translated in an article written "following Dupont-Sommer" (*Le Flambeau*, No. 1, 1956, p. 47).

At Qumran the two meanings are both attested to in the three other passages in which the term is used:

Hymns, VIII, 16

Thou, O my God, hast placed in my mouth as it were a freshet of the autumn rain. (In Palestine the autumn rain is the one most desired and which does the most good.)

Damascus Document, III, 8

They (the Israelites of the Exodus) did not obey the voice of their Creator, [the] voice of their instructor. (This would mean God or Moses.)

Damascus Document, XX, 14

From the day of the disappearance of the Instructor of the Community . . . (Here we are clearly dealing with the Teacher of Righteousness.)

A particularly curious case occurs in the *Damascus Document*, XIX, 35 and XX, 1. The scribe first began by writing YWRH, then crossed it out to replace it with MWRH, which he again crossed out, finally carrying over this same MWRH, to the succeeding line. This demonstrates that the two terms could be confused with one another, but that the copyists did not consider them to be equivalent words.

Fortunately, our text of the *Damascus Document* is not subject to this confusion here, as it is manifestly a reference to *Hosea* 10:12:

> Sow to yourselves in righteousness,
> reap in mercy;
> break up your fallow ground;
> for it is time to seek Yahweh,
> till he come and rain righteousness upon you.

In this agricultural context, where he speaks of seedtime and harvest and plowing, we cannot doubt that the prophet Hosea means by the term the autumn rain, so eagerly awaited after the torrid heat of the Palestinian summer. Indeed, in the context of the *Damascus Document*, an opposition is made between those who in olden times had to dig a (symbolic) pit in order to find there the water of the Law, and those who at the end of time will receive without effort the rain of righteousness. Consequently, we ought to translate it like this: "until he shall arise who will make righteousness rain down at the end of days." The Old Testament so often compares the messianic salvation to the effects of a refreshing rain (*Ps.* 72:6; *Isa.* 45:8; *Hos.* 6:3 and 10:2; *Joel* 2:23; *Ecclus.* 35:26) that the men of Qumran, nourished on the Bible as they were,[11] could hardly fail to seize upon this allusion and to appreciate its appeal to a Biblical image.[12]

Thus, the examination of the *Habakkuk Commentary* V, 3-5, and the *Damascus Document* VI, 10-11, shows us how tenuous are any conclusions drawn from these texts. In point of fact, we have no single valid proof that the Essenes believed in the special intervention of the Teacher

[11] See, for instance, "Les Citations de l'Ancien Testament dans la Guerre des Fils de Lumière . . ." *Revue Biblique*, 1956, No. 2, pp. 234–60 and No. 3, pp. 375–90; and "Les Citations de l'Ancien Testament, et spécialement des Poèmes du Serviteur, dans les Hymnes de Qumrân," *Revue de Qumrân*, no. 7, pp. 357–94.

[12] With the vanishing of any argument based on this text in favor of the final return of the Teacher of Righteousness disappears also another argument in favor of his messiahship. Dupont-Sommer has put his case thus:

"*During the whole time of the wickedness until the coming of the Teacher of Righteousness at the end of the days.*" This text is fundamental. In fact, a close parallel between this formula, and the other which has been quoted above—"*during the time of the wickedness until the coming of the Anointed of Aaron and Israel*" (XII, 23)—suggests without any doubt whatsoever that "the Anointed of Aaron and Israel" is the Teacher of Righteousness

of Righteousness either at the Last Judgment as the one who would mete out punishment to the heathen nations, or during the messianic era as the bringer of lasting peace on earth.

On this point also the comparison between Christ and the Teacher of Righteousness fails. Concerning the Teacher we have merely hypotheses without any assured foundation; concerning Christ, we have the formal witness of the Gospels as to His resurrection and the oft-repeated promise of a glorious return "to judge the quick and the dead." Furthermore, may it not be because the Christian creed so stresses this article that there has been an attempt to introduce it also into that of the Essenes?

5. *Summary of* all *texts concerning the Teacher*

Having considered these matters in so much detail, we should now bring together all the information we have concerning the Teacher of Righteousness so as to build up a complete picture. Here, then, is a review of *all* the texts actually known, which speak, explicitly or implicitly, of the Master so revered by the Essenes.

Habakkuk Commentary

"[   ] it is the Teacher of Righteousness [   ] . . ." (I, 13).

"[   ] the traitors with the Man of Lies, for they belie[ved]

---

himself" (*Jewish Sect of Qumrân and the Essenes*, p. 54).

But if the former text merely refers to him who shall make righteousness fall like rain, the similarity between these two passages shows only that the "rain" of righteousness should be attributed to "the Anointed of Aaron and Israel," or rather (see above pp. 23-27) to the Anointed of Israel, because of the palpable influence of *Psalm* 72:6 with its attribution of this very action to "the King's son."

not [the words of][1] the Teacher of Righteousness from the mouth of God" (II, 1-3).

"These are the vio[lent ones . . .][2] who will not believe when they hear all the things which will happ[en in] the last generation from the mouth of the priest[3] whom God placed in [the house of Jud]ah to explain all the words of His servants, the prophets (II, 6–8).

The explanation of this refers to the House of Absalom and its supporters who were silent when the Teacher of Righteousness was punished[4] and did not aid him against the Man of Untruth (V, 9-11).

As for what is said "so he may run who reads it"[5] this applies to the Teacher of Righteousness whom God made to know all the mysteries of the words of His servants, the prophets (VII, 3-5).

The explanation of this refers to all those who practice the Law in the House of Judah, whom God will deliver from the House of Judgment because of their affliction and their faith[6] in the Teacher of Righteousness (VIII, 1-3).

[   ] struck by him in the execution of iniquitous judgments; and odious profaners committed horrors on him and vengeance on his body of flesh (IX, 1-2).[7]

[1] Restoration proposed by Dupont-Sommer.

[2] All the restorations in this passage are proposed by Dupont-Sommer.

[3] This "priest" is undoubtedly the Teacher of Righteousness.

[4] A vague enough term; one that could mean discussion, argument, trial, judgment, rebuke, or punishment.

[5] The complete text of *Habakkuk* 2:2 reads: "Write the vision; make it plain upon tablets, so he may run who reads it."

[6] An unusual term (*Nehemiah* 10:1, 11:23, and *Damascus Document*, XX, 12), whose meaning is hard to determine precisely. One hesitates between belief, confidence, assurance.

[7] Translation of Dupont-Sommer, who applies this passage to the Teacher of Righteousness. On the other hand, M. Michel applies it to the Wicked Priest and translates: "To strike him in the afflictions of his ungodliness and of horrible things",—that is to say, he has been made to suffer from pernicious ailments as well as from vengeance committed on his body of flesh" (*Le Maître de Justice*, p. 14).

This means the Wicked Priest, whom, for the wrong done to the Teacher of Righteousness and the men of his party, God delivered into the hands of his enemies, afflicting him with a destroying scourge, in bitterness of soul, because he acted wickedly against His elect (IX, 9-12).[8]

This means the wicked priest, who persecuted the Teacher of Righteousness in order to confound him in the indignation of his wrath, wishing to banish him; and at the time of their festival of rest, the day of atonement, he appeared to them to confound them and to make them stumble on the day of fasting, their Sabbath of rest (XI, 4-8).

Micah Commentary

[This applies to the] Teacher of Righteousness, who is [the instructor of the Law for] his [council] and for those who offer themselves to join the elect ones of [God, who practise the Law] in the counsel of the Comunity, who [will] be saved from the day of [   ] (8: 10, 6: 9).[9]

Commentary on Psalm 37

This applies to the priest, the Teacher of [Righteousness whom] he has established to build for him the congregation of [his elect (ones)][10] (*Fragment I*, II, 15-16.)[11]

This applies to the Wicked [Prie]st who s[ent to the Teacher of Righteousness   ] in order to slay him [   ] and the Law, which he sent to him. But God will not le[ave him in his hand] nor [condemn him when] he is judged.[12] And [God will] repay to [him] his recompense to give him into

[8] Or "His elect (ones)," if we suppose an abnormal spelling of the plural.

[9] *Qumran Cave I*, No. 14, p. 78. The restorations adopted are those of the editor, J. T. Milik.

[10] One could also suppose here "the poor."

[11] Fragment edited and restored by Allegro: *Palestine Exploration Quarterly*, No. 2, 1954, p. 71.

[12] Citation from *Ps.* 37:33, which the commentator is about to explain.

the hand of terrible ones of the Gentiles to do to him [. . .][13] (*Fragment II*, 2-4).[14]

Damascus Document

They (the Remnant of Israel) were like men blind and groping for the way[15] for twenty years. And God observed their works, that they sought him with a perfect heart; and he raised up for them a Teacher of Righteousness to lead them in the way of his heart (I, 9-11).[16]

From the day of the disappearance of the Teacher of the Community until there shall arise the anointed [issue] of Aaron and [issue] of Israel (XIX, 35-XX, 1).[17]

From the day of disappearance of the Instructor of the Community until the destruction of all the men of war who followed after the man of untruth (XX, 13-15).

All those who are strengthened in these commandments to do[18] in all things according to the Law, and (who) obeyed the voice of the Teacher and who confessed before God: "We have sinned, both we and our fathers" (XX, 27-29).

[Those who] shall be instructed in the first commandments by which the men of the community[19] were ruled, [who] shall have lent the ear to the voice of the Teacher of Righteousness, [who] shall not have answered [contrary to] the decrees of righteousness when they shall have heard them (XX, 31-33).

Reading these passages, *which are the only ones we actually possess concerning the Teacher of Righteousness,* we recognize the extremely tenuous quality of our infor-

---

[13] This last sentence seems to refer to the Wicked Priest rather than to the Teacher of Righteousness.

[14] Fragment edited and restored by Allegro, (*Journal of Biblical Literature*, June, 1956, p. 94).

[15] Allusion to *Isa.* 59:10.

[16] Translation of Millar Burrows (Translator's note).

[17] See p. 22 and the explanation given on pp. 23-24, and 64-65.

[18] Literally, "to go in and out."

[19] Here again the scribe has confused *yahad* ("community") with *yahid* ("unique"), or *yihud* ("uniqueness").

mation—one passage of a few words almost without meaning, six whose gaps make interpretation difficult, ten allusions which are clearer—but all of them so brief and altogether so incomplete!

Yet these are the texts on which have been built such formidable conclusions. These are the texts that have led some writers to discover in the Teacher of Righteousness, "the perfect mediator between man and God" (Allegro, *The Dead Sea Scrolls*, p. 149); "the Messiah redeemer of the world" (Dupont-Sommer, *The Dead Sea Scrolls; a Preliminary Survey*, p. 99); a being more or less deified, a "savior crucified and risen again," whose adherents fervently awaited His glorious return" (*Ibid.*, p. 99). These are the texts which inspired Dupont-Sommer to write:

Of the Teacher of Righteousness, whose career preceded that of the Galilean Rabbi by about a century, we knew practically nothing until now . . . Everything is now changed, and all the problems relative to primitive Christianity—problems earnestly examined for so many centuries—all these problems henceforth find themselves placed in a new light, which forces us to reconsider them completely (*Ibid.*, p. 100).

The enthusiasm accorded this "revolution"—or rather, this "whole cascade of revolutions" (*Ibid.*, p. 96)—is astonishing. "It does not seem," proclaims Professor Étiemble, "that any new fact will ever be able to weaken a demonstration so rigorously proven that it is hardly open to question" (*Temps Modernes*, 1951, p. 1287).

On the other hand, it is not surprising that the enthusiasm of the best scholars in the field concerning these "discoveries" was considerably less ecstatic. C. G. Howie gives it as his opinion that "Never have a few writers drawn so many conclusions from so little evidence as has been done in the comparisons of Jesus and the Teacher of

Righteousness" (*The Dead Sea Scrolls and the Living Church*, 1958, p. 107).

And Allegro's fellow-workers in the Jerusalem "Scrollery" felt obliged to protest certain of his findings:

It has come to our attention that considerable controversy is being caused by certain broadcast statements of Mr. John Allegro, of the University of Manchester, concerning the Dead Sea Scrolls. We refer particularly to such statements as imply that in these scrolls a close connexion is to be found between a supposed crucifixion and Resurrection of Jesus Christ. The announced opinions of Mr. Allegro might seem to have special weight, since he is one of the group of scholars engaged in editing as yet unpublished writings from Qumran.

In view of the broad repercussions of his statements and the fact that the materials on which they are based are not yet available to the public, we, his colleagues, feel obliged to make the following statement. There are no unpublished texts at the disposal of Mr. Allegro other than those of which the originals are at present in the Palestine Archaeological Museum where we are working. Upon the appearance in the press of citations from Mr. Allegro's broadcasts we have reviewed all the pertinent materials, published and unpublished. We are unable to see in the texts the "findings" of Mr. Allegro.

We find no crucifixion of the "teacher," no deposition from the cross, and no "broken body of their Master" to be stood guard over until Judgment Day. Therefore there is no "well defined Essenic (see note 8 on p. 11) pattern into which Jesus of Nazareth fits," as Mr. Allegro is alleged in one report to have said. It is our conviction that either he has misread the Texts or he has built up a chain of conjectures which the materials do not support (*Time* magazine, Feb. 6, 1956, p. 88).[20]

And here is the opinion of Professor H. H. Rowley,

[20] This protest is signed by "Roland de Vaux, O.P., J. T. Milik, P. W. Skehan, Jean Starcky, John Strugnell."

known throughout the world not only for the quality of his scholarship but for the courtesy and moderation of his judgments, on his former student, Allegro:

I deplore as unscholarly the presentation to the world of what scholars everywhere have supposed—as I supposed—to be specific statements in an unpublished text to which Mr. Allegro alone had access, when they are only his deductions from evidence which is capable of other interpretations. . . . Mr. Allegro was one of the most promising students I have ever had, and he is capable of doing fine work. I think it is a pity that he was entrusted with the editing of texts far from supervision. . . . Important documents, for which scholars in all countries are eagerly waiting, should not be used to give immature scholars a spurious authority (*Time*, April 2, 1956, p. 71).

Need we add that the staff writer who reported this statement chose as the title of his article, *Teacher Spanks?*

III

Christ and the Teacher Compared: Their Works and Doctrine

1. Conduct

AFTER STUDYING the arguments advanced by Dupont-
Sommer and Allegro, and examining all the texts
that constitute our real information, we see that Christ
was not a mere "reincarnation" of the Teacher of Righteousness, that He was not content just to slip into a pre-
existing role, that His life was not dominated by a concern
to "copy" His so-called "predecessor."

Nevertheless, the extreme positions taken by certain
writers ought not to deter us from a dispassionate consideration of the possible resemblances between the mind
of Christ and the thinking of the Essenes. In the plan of
God the Old Testament was the preparation for the New.
It would be strange if the Essene sect—the noblest of the
religious movements born of Judaism—had not also had
its providential place in the perfecting of souls and the
evolution of ideas in preparing the way for the message of
the Son of God.

This problem, which involves the very *selves* of the two
religious leaders and covers the whole of the works they
accomplished, needs a scientific method of research. The
fact is that both Essenism and Christianity have their

roots in the Old Testament, and therefore the presence in each of Biblical elements is no proof of reciprocal influence. Moreover, several related streams of thought flowed together in the Palestine of Christ's time; so a precise study must distinguish carefully between the elements common among these diverse currents and the traits characteristic of each spiritual family.

Hence, if we wish to proceed in scholarly fashion, as soon as we have identified a real likeness between Christianity and Essenism we ought to examine the position of the Old Testament on the point, and also that of the other Jewish "sects," the Pharisees and the Sadducees. If the likeness is a trait characteristic of the Essenes only, the comparison will be useful and instructive; but if it proves to be an element borrowed from the common patrimony of Judaism, the resemblance will be insufficient to establish a true kinship between Christianity and Essenism.

Thus, for example, we read in the *Rule of the Community*, V, 24-VI, 1, that

In order to reprove one another in t[rut]h, humility and kindly love for each; that one shall not speak to his [brother] in anger, or in faultfinding, or in stubbo[rness or in the   ] of a wicked spirit; that he shall not hate him [for the uncircumcision of] his heart; thus, the day [when] he shall have reproved him he shall not bring upon him any evil; likewise, let no one bring his case against another before the Masters until after a rebuke before witnesses.[1]

Obviously, this text is reminiscent of those in the New Testament concerning brotherly correction:

If your brother sins against you, go and tell him his fault, between you and him alone. If he listens to you, you have

[1] This last phrase is reproduced almost literally in the *Damascus Document*, IX, 3.

gained your brother. But if he does not listen, take one or two others along with you, that every word may be confirmed by the evidence of two or three witnesses.[2] If he refuses to listen to them, tell (it) to the church (*Matt.* 18:15-17).

If your brother sins, rebuke him, and if he repents, forgive him (*Luke* 17:3).

If a man is overtaken in any trespass, you who are spiritual, should forgive him (*Gal.* 6:1).

But the fact is that the text of *The Rule of the Community* does no more than paraphrase *Leviticus* 19:17,

You shall not hate your brother in your heart, but you shall reason with your neighbor, lest you bear sin because of him.

Official Judaism likewise attached great importance to this prohibition of *Leviticus*, citing and commenting on it frequently[3]; hence we have no right to state that Christianity depends for this tenet on Essenism, for it may be another parallel application of the Old Testament (*Matthew* 18:16 is an exact quotation from *Deuteronomy* 19:15), or else it may reflect a current practice in Judaism.

In making this necessarily critical approach to our sources, we can and should recognize that Essenism certainly prepared souls for the message of Christ, deepening genuine piety and sincere love of God, and encouraging a commendable concern for moral perfection. If the *Hymns* of Qumran were known to the public, they must have developed and refined the religious sensibilities of many a reader and may perhaps have led several to a real awareness of God's presence. And even if the Essene works rarely left the houses of the sect, the sight of the pious and dedicated lives of these courageous anchorites

[2] Reference to *Deut.* 19:15.

[3] See Strack-Billerbeck, *Kommentar zum Neuen Testament aus Talmud und Midrash,* I, 787–92; IV, 1286.

could not fail to encourage a spirit of other-worldliness and a climate of collective fervor.

For a clear understanding of the relations between Essenism and Christianity they should be viewed under three different aspects: the characteristic behavior of the Essenes, their peculiar doctrines, and the literary expression of their works.

Since the Essenes were not all limited to Qumran or to places of inaccessible solitude, the inhabitants of Palestine, on the whole, would have been roughly acquainted with their rites, their customs, their way of life; it is even possible that many people entertained a sincere and entirely justified admiration for them. As a consequence we might expect that in many details Jesus and His disciples would have imitated their example and assumed their virtues.

a) MARRIAGE AND CHASTITY

Although the official documents of Essenism look favorably on marriage (*Damascus Document*, VII, 6-9; *Rule for the Whole Congregation of Israel*, I, 4, 9-11 in *Qumrân Cave I*, No. 28a, p. 109), the obsession with legal impurity[4] and probably also the intensity of their religious fervor developed, in practice, a habit of absolute continence, which was a cause of much wonder to the ancient historians Philo of Alexandria, Pliny the Elder, and Flavius Josephus. Obviously, this development of chastity could have exerted some influence on the virginal marriage of the Blessed Virgin and St. Joseph, on the celibacy of Paul and Barnabas (*I Cor.* 9:5-6), and on the ideal of perfect

[4] The Jewish Law provided that contact with certain people or objects considered as "impure" would make one contract a sort of blemish which rendered one unfit for performing certain religious acts, although this "legal impurity" did not constitute a sin, properly speaking.

chastity which progressively won the allegiance of un-selfish souls (*I Cor.* 7:1-40; *Apoc.* 14:1-5).

Despite the explicit permissions of the Old Testament and the constant usage of Judaism, the Essenes con-demned polygamy. The *Damascus Document* (IV, 20-V, 2) places among the three chief snares of Belial "lust, (which means) taking two women during their life, when the basis of creation is that 'male and female He created them' (*Gen.* I:27), when those who went into the ark went in two by two (*Gen.* 6:20 and 7:2, 8-9, 15-16), and when it is written concerning the ruler that 'he shall not multiply wives for himself' (*Deut.* 17:7)." The taking of such a stand must have been known to the "general public" and clearly prepared for the Christian doctrine of marriage (*Matt.* 19:3-12).

b) THE SPIRITUALITY OF THE DESERT

When St. John the Baptist, Jesus, and St. Paul withdrew *into the desert,* they were surely obedient to a deep in-stinct rooted in the Old Testament, that goes back as far as Elijah and beyond him to the Exodus; but they were, in fact, acting in accord also with the example given them by the men of Qumran, who were, among their con-temporaries, the principal exponents of "the spirituality of the desert." And the survivors of Essenism, escaping the massacre of the Roman legions, were able to transmit certain of their traditions to the first ascetics of Christian monasticism.

When Jesus sent His disciples out to preach, He directed them:

Take no gold, nor silver, nor copper in your belts, no bag for your journey, nor two tunics, nor sandals, nor a staff; for the laborer deserves his food. And whatever town or village you enter, find out who is worthy in it, and stay with him until you depart (*Matt.* 10:9-11).

Actually, these directions amount to saying, "Behave like the Essenes," since these people, according to Josephus, practised a similar unconcern for worldly matters.

And if any of their sect come from other places, what they have lies open for them, just as if it were their own, and they go into such as they never knew before, as if they had been ever so long acquainted with them. For which reason they carry nothing at all with them when they travel into remote parts, though still they take their weapons with them, for fear of thieves. Accordingly, there is, in every city where they live, one appointed particularly to take care of strangers, and to provide garments and other necessaries for them (*Jewish Wars*, II, VIII, 4, 124-26).

c) THE SWEARING OF OATHS

Whereas the rabbinical writings testify to an unfortunate tendency to swear a great many oaths, the Essenes were reluctant to do this—or at least they substituted for the oath by the name of God the oath by the "curses of the Covenant" (*Damascus Document*, XV, 1-10; XVI, 10-12; *Rule of the Community*, II, 1-18; V, 8). So, says Josephus, "whatsoever they say is firmer than an oath, but swearing is avoided by them, and they esteem it worse than perjury, for they say that he who cannot be believed without (swearing by) God is already condemned" (*Jewish Wars* II, VIII, 6:135).

Jesus approved this reaction and adopted a similar attitude:

You have heard that it was said to the men of old, "You shall not swear falsely, but shall perform to the Lord whatever you have sworn." But I say to you, do not swear at all, whether

78

by heaven, for it is the throne of God, or by the earth, for it is His footstool, or by Jerusalem, for it is the city of the great King. And do not swear by your head, for you cannot make one hair white or black. Let what you say be simply "Yes" or "No"; anything more than this comes from evil (*Matt.* 5:33-37).

d) THE IDEAL OF POVERTY

Jesus chose for Himself a "style of living" that was as poor and as unworldly as that of the Essenes, and like them He applied Himself to manual labor. Moreover, after His death the Christians of Jerusalem would realize this ideal of poverty, modeling themselves on the Essene methods:

Now the company of those who believed were of one heart and soul, and no one said that any of the things which he possessed was his own, but they had everything in common . . . there was not a needy person among them, for as many as were possessors of lands or houses sold them, and brought the proceeds of what was sold and laid it at the Apostles' feet; and distribution was made to each as any had need (*Acts* 4:32-35).

This was in fact the spontaneous application of a practice codified in the *Rule of the Community*. When the novice has been tested for a year,

his wealth and his wages shall be put at the disposal of the man who has supervision over the wages of the Masters; he shall enter it in the account at his disposal, but shall not spend it for the Masters.

Then, a year later, the novice is admitted and registered "among his brethren" for law, and for judgment and for the purification and for the sharing of his property . . ." (*Rule of the Community* VI, 19-20, 22). Nevertheless,

79

certain differences exist. At Qumran the community of goods is obligatory, whereas in the Jerusalem Church it is optional (*Acts* 5:1-11).[5] However, the fraud of Ananias and Saphira is punished by a spectacular death (*Acts*, 5:1-11), whereas among the Essenes "if there is found among them a man who lies about his wealth, and knows it, he shall be excluded from the purification of the Masters for a year, and shall be deprived of a fourth of his food ration" (*Rule of the Community*, VI:24-25).

e) ADMINISTRATIVE ORGANIZATION

Within Judaism the Sadducees and the Pharisees were constituted more like spiritual "families" than well structured "societies." The Essenes, on the other hand, achieved really homogeneous *organizations*, with a detailed legislation and with officers vested with strict authority. To describe this new reality they employed the term *yahad*, "community," which was almost unknown in the Old Testament[6] and which corresponds perfectly to the Greek *koinônia*, used some twenty times in the *Acts of the Apostles* and the *Epistles*. In fact, Jesus conceived His church—and the Apostles developed it—very much according to the Essene "type," with general regulations that would go on developing in more and more detail, with an authority constituted by Peter and the Apostles, followed by the deacons and "elders." Certainly, Christ took care

[5] Canon Osty points out that this ideal of poverty is presented with a special insistence by St. Luke. In addition to the passages cited from the *Acts*, see *Luke* 5:11, compared with *Matt.* 4:22, and *Mark* 1:20; *Luke* 18:22, compared with *Matt.* 19:21, and *Mark* 10:21; *Luke* 12:23 compared with *Matt.* 6:19; *Luke* 14:33. Would Luke have been more susceptible to Essene influence? Or did this emphasis, perhaps, agree more closely with his own personal aspirations?

[6] See on the other hand the study by S. Talmon in *Vetus Testamentum*, No. 2, 1953, pp. 133–40.

to leave to His "community" more flexibility, and thus more capacity for adaptation and growth than we find any evidence of in the more rigid, and shorter-lived, Essene community; we can hardly deny, however, that He contemplated for His disciples a very definite "organization," one that would naturally copy that of the Essenes up to a certain point.[7]

f) FRATERNITY AND COMMUNITY OF GOODS

In communities such as that of Qumran the members observed a spirit of perfect *fraternity*, and the newest were treated as well as those who exercised the authority. According to Josephus,

These men are despisers of riches, and so very communicative as raises our admiration. Nor is there anyone to be found among them who hath more than another; for it is a law among them, that those who have come to them must let what they have be common to the whole order, insomuch that among them all there is no appearance of poverty, or excess of riches, but every one's possessions are intermingled with every other's possessions, and so there is, as it were, one patrimony among all the brethren (*Jewish Wars*, II, VIII, 3:122).

And, in Philo's testimony,

They who live together and share the same table are content with the same things every day, being lovers of frugality, and abhorring prodigality as a disease of soul and body. Not only have they a common table, but also common raiment (*Apology for the Jews*, 11-12).

There is not a single slave among them; all are free and exchange kind offices with each other. They condemn the

[7] See, for example, *Matt.* 16:18–19; *Luke* 22:32; *John* 21:16–17; *Acts* 1:23–26; 2:42; 6:1–6; etc.

position of master, not only as unjust, being a breach of equality, but as impious, since it violates the order of Mother Nature, which gives birth to all alike and rears them as genuine brothers, not as nominal (Philo, *Quod Omnis Probus Liber Sit,* 79).

These descriptions have an evangelical flavor; they agree well with the directive of Jesus: "You are all brethren . . . he who is greatest among you shall be your servant" (*Matt.* 23:8, 11); and they are in accord with the views of Saint Paul: "For as many of you as were baptized into Christ have put on Christ. There is neither Jew nor Greek, there is neither slave nor free, there is neither male nor female; for you are all one in Christ Jesus" (*Gal.* 3:27-28).

g) THE CALENDAR

The Essene writings insist often on the respect due the traditional calendar (*Rule of the Community,* I:13-15; X:3-8; *Damascus Document,* III:14-15; VI:18-19; XVI:2-4; *Sayings of Moses,* I:8;[8] a whole section of the book of *Enoch,* chapters 72-82; and the book of *Jubilees* generally). This seems to correspond to the ancient biblical usage, although from the beginning of the second century B.C. the official cult had been celebrated according to a different calendar, one of Hellenistic origin.[9] Now this difference may possibly resolve the problem of the date of the Last Supper,[10] placed by the synoptic Gospels as the night following the sacrifice of the paschal lamb at the Temple, and by St. John as preceding that event. If our

[8] This text has been published in *Qumran Cave I,* No. 22, p. 92.

[9] A. Jaubert, "Le calendrier des Jubilés et de la secte de Qumran; ses origines bibliques," *Vetus Testamentum,* No. 3, (1953), pp. 250–64.

[10] A. Jaubert, "La date de la dernière Cène," *Revue de l'Histoire des Religions,* 146 (October-December, 1954), 140-73; and more recently, her complete book, *La Date de la Cène, calendrier biblique et liturgie chrétienne,* (Paris, 1957).

Lord had followed the Essene calendar, both accounts could be correct. But we do not know whether other groups followed this usage, nor would such a practice necessarily presuppose direct influence from Essenism, since it could also be merely a survival from the traditional Biblical calendar.[11]

However this may be, the Essenes did not deny the worship of the Jerusalem Temple[12]; but their differences over the calendar and their contempt for the high priestly class currently functioning kept them for the time being cut off from the official ceremonies. In this they anticipated, after a fashion, the abandonment of this worship and its ultimate replacement by the sacrifice of Christ. But the attitude of Jesus and his disciples was markedly different from that of the Essenes. The latter admitted in theory the traditional liturgy but were cool toward it in practice; while the first Christians, on the contrary, did not refuse to frequent the Temple although they considered its sacrifices as peripheral.

Alongside these positive resemblances, however, we find differences amounting to actual opposition.

h) SABBATH OBSERVANCE

Thus, as regards the Sabbath—the rigidity of the Essenes may be judged from the following rules:

[11] A. Jaubert, "Le Calendrier des Jubilés et les jours liturgiques de la semaine," Vetus Testamentum, No. 1, 1957, pp. 35–61.

[12] See "L'utilité ou l'inutilité des sacrifices sanglants dans la Règle de la Communauté de Qumrân," Revue Biblique, No. 4, 1956, pp. 524–32. The conclusions of this article have since been confirmed by the publication of a new text, edited by Allegro: "He (God) shall be seen continually upon it (the sanctuary), and strangers shall not again make it desolate as they desolated formerly the sanc[tuary of I]srael because of their sin. And he purposed to build for him a man-made sanctuary in which sacrifices might be made to him; [that there might be] before him works of the Law" (J. M. Allegro, Journal of Biblical Literature, No. 4, 1958, p. 352).

Let no one speak of the work and the labor to be done the next morning. . . . Let no one eat or drink anything except what is to be found in the camp. . . . Let no one put on garments that are filthy or have come from storage unless they have been washed with water or rubbed with incense. . . . Let no one lift his hand to strike [a beast] with his fist. . . . Let no one open a sealed vessel on the Sabbath. Let no one carry ointments on him, going and coming on the Sabbath. . . . Let not the nurse carry the suckling child going and coming on the Sabbath. . . . Let no one help an animal to give birth on the Sabbath day; and if it falls into a well or a ditch, let no one lift it out on the Sabbath. . . . And if any person falls into a place full of water, let no one bring him up by a ladder or rope or instrument (*Damascus Document*, X, 19-XI, 17).

If we compare such interdictions with the attitude of Jesus—who proclaimed that the Sabbath was made for man and not man for the Sabbath (*Mark* 2:27); who commended those who would rescue an ass or an ox from a pit even on the Sabbath day (*Luke* 14:5); who healed a sick man and sent him on his way with his litter precisely on the Sabbath (*John* 5:8-10)—we appreciate the enormous distance separating Christianity from Essenism. Jesus conserved only the religious value of the weekly day of rest, while the Essenes exceeded even the rigors of the Mosaic Law and Jewish casuistry.

i) RITUAL PURITY

The Essenes were obsessed by a concern for *legal purity*, so as not to defile the presence of God and the angels in their midst: "For holy angels are in their congregation" (*The Rule of the Congregation*, II, 8-9). "For the angels of holiness are with their armies" (*War Scroll* VIII, 6). "[The priests] shall not go amongst the slain, lest they defile themselves in their impure blood, for they are holy; they shall not profane the oil of the anointing of their priesthood in the blood of the nations of the void" (*War Scroll*, IX:7-9).

Consequently, even more scrupulously than other Jews, they avoided eating or drinking with the ungodly (*Rule of the Community*, V:16), or letting their goods come in contact with those of the latter (*Ibid.*, IX:8-9), or sending offerings to the Temple carried by an unclean man (*Damascus Document*, XI:18-20), or enjoying the marriage relation in the city of the sanctuary, making it unclean with their impurity (*Damascus Document*, XII:1-2).

Let not a man make himself abominable with any living creature or creeping thing by eating of them, from the larvae of bees to any living creature that creeps in the water. And let not fish be eaten unless they have been split alive and their blood has been poured out. And all the locusts according to their kinds shall be put into fire or into water while they are still alive, for this is the law of their creation. And all wood and stones and dust which are polluted by the uncleanness of men. . . . according to their uncleanness he who touches them shall be unclean (*Damascus Document* XII: 11-17).

Accordingly the Essenes took great care to multiply their ritual purifications in order to expunge all these impurities. And therefore, even more than other Jews, they would have been profoundly shocked to see the disciples of Jesus eat without even washing their hands (*Matt.* 15:2), and to hear Jesus Himself proclaim the inefficacy of these legal observances (*Ibid.*, 15:3-20). On this point Jesus held a position exactly opposed to Jewish practice, and even more so to Essene scruples.[13]

[13] This explains, perhaps, why the Gospel never mentions the Essenes, who would never have been willing to mingle with the crowds who gathered about the Galilean "prophet," and were therefore voluntarily protected from coming under His influence.

To sum up, we can show that Jesus, like all His disciples and hearers, knew the outward forms of Essene observances, and agreed with them sometimes in their application of certain righteous qualities, but that He felt free to oppose them whenever their excesses negated genuine moral values, and especially that He created a radical new attitude in His disciples by substituting His own authority for that of Moses.

2. Sacraments

At this point, two special cases need to be studied in greater detail because of the contradictory opinions they have provoked. Since the men of Qumran multiplied ritual washings and met together to eat in common, certain writers immediately talk of "sacraments" comparable to the Christian ones. "These daily baptisms and communal meals," says Dupont-Sommer, "are the two principal rites and basic sacraments of the Sect of the Covenant" (*The Jewish Sect of Qumran and the Essenes*, pp. 97-98).

a) BAPTISMS OR ABLUTIONS?

Obsessed constantly by the fear of legal impurities, the Essenes were most careful to purify themselves by the ablutions prescribed in the Old Testament (see, for example, chapters 11 and 15 of *Leviticus* and 19 of *Num-*

Jesus, on the other hand, knowing the virtue of these holy people, would doubtless have thought it better to leave them to their good faith and not to expose His Church to their intransigence. But the facts set forth in this chapter show clearly that Jesus was not ignorant concerning them.

bers). In this they were in full accord with the current practice of the Jews:

For the Pharisees, and all the Jews, do not eat unless they wash their hands, observing the tradition of the elders; and when they come from the market place, they do not eat unless they purify themselves; and there are many other traditions which they observe, the washing of cups and pots and vessels of bronze (*Mark* 7:3-4. See also *Matt.* 15:2, and *John* 2:6).

But the Essenes attached such an importance to this practice that it formed a punishment among them to be deprived of it.

(The unrighteous) is not to go into water in order to attain the purity of holy men (*Rule of the Community*, V, 13).

Let (the candidate) not come into the purification of the Masters until after he has been examined (*Ibid.*, VI, 16-17).

Let (the transgressor) be kept away from the purification of the Masters for a year (*Ibid.*, VI, 25).[1]

Thus, for the Essenes, admission to the "purifications" became in some sort a kind of "setting apart" into the Community, just as baptism was the entering step among the disciples of John or those of Christ. But is this sufficient argument for identifying these ablutions with the baptism of John, or even with Christian baptism?

The Essenes saw in them more than a merely symbolic

[1] See also VII:3, 16, 19, VIII:17, 24. If laymen, novices and evil-doers were thus excluded from the "purification of the Masters," it was doubtless because of fear lest contact with these impure persons should be sufficient to defile the water in which the true "men of holiness" purified themselves. In similar fashion Josephus tells us that if an old member touched a new one he had to purify himself as if after contact with a stranger (*Jewish Wars* II, VIII, 10,150).

action, and they insisted, if the rites were to be efficacious, on a proper inward state of mind.

[The man of obstinate heart] shall not become innocent through expiations, he shall not be purified by the cleansing waters, he shall not be sanctified by seas and rivers, he shall not be purified by all the waters of ablution; impure, impure shall he be all the days of his disdain towards the decrees of God . . . (*Rule of the Community*, III, 4-6).

But in the case of the faithful Essene,

through the submission of his soul to all the precepts of God, his flesh shall be purified by the sprinkling of cleansing waters and by the sanctification of the rushing stream (*Ibid.*, 8-9).

This insistence on a close adherence to the ordinances of God is not without a certain resemblance to the profound "conversion" that accompanied the baptisms of John and of Jesus.

But in spite of this fact, the ablutions of the men of Qumran still remained in the line of traditional Judaism, whereas the baptisms of John and of Jesus differed radically from it. The Essenes, like all Jews, performed these washings for themselves, but baptism was administered by John, or by the disciples of Jesus (*John* 4:2). Ablutions among the Essenes, and all other Jews, were repeated daily, to cleanse from routine contaminations; but baptism was conferred once only, and in a decisive fashion. Ablutions, for the Essenes and for all Jews, were a logical consequence of the extreme importance attached to the legal purity of the body; but John took no account of these *minutiae* (*Luke* 3:7-14), and Jesus declared that defilement came only from within.

Furthermore, the people of the time do not seem to have been under any misapprehension concerning John's baptism. The crowds from "Jerusalem, and all Judaea, and all the region round about Jordan" (*Matt.* 3:5) who flocked to receive this rite would hardly have been captivated by a mere imitator of the Essenes whom they had long known about. The numerous Pharisees and Sadducees (*Matt.* 3:7) who were won over by this enthusiasm, would not have come to submit themselves to a rite inspired by their adversaries, the Essenes. Furthermore, to silence the high priests and the elders, Jesus put to them exactly the question that we are considering:

"The baptism of John, whence was it? from Heaven, or of men?" And they reasoned with themselves, saying: "If we shall say, 'From Heaven,' he will say unto us, 'Why did ye not then believe him?' But if we shall say, 'Of men,' we fear the people; for all hold John as a prophet. And they answered Jesus, and said, "We cannot tell" (*Matt.* 21:25-27).

If John had done no more than accommodate himself to an Essene practice, he would not have aroused so much sympathy among the people nor caused such embarrassment in higher circles.

In summary, we can say that even though the ablutions of the Essenes were more than a purely exterior rite, and even though they attested a particular affiliation to the Community, they retained the essential traits of traditional Jewish practice, and thus they belonged to an altogether different order from both the baptism "of conversion" administered by John and the baptism "in the name of the Father and of the Son, and of the Holy Spirit" (*Matt.* 28:19) instituted by Jesus.

b) COMMUNAL MEAL OR SACRAMENTAL COMMUNION?

The Essene meals are known to us from several sources.

When the table shall have been prepared for eating, or the wine for drinking, the priest shall first extend his hand to bless the first portions of bread or of wine[2] (*Rule of the Community* VI:4-6).

This is the order of the session of "men of renown called to the assembly"[3] for the counsel of the Community, if [God] brings the Anointed (one) to birth[4] among them: There shall come the chief [priest] of the whole congregation of Israel and all the f[athers, the sons of] Aaron, the priests, "called to the assembly, men of renown" and they shall seat themselves be[fore him, each] in proportion to his dignity; next [shall be seat]ed [the Anointed] of Israel and before him shall be seated the heads[5] of the th[ousands of Israel ea]ch in proportion to his dignity, according to [his] p[lace] in their camps and according to their [orders of] departure[6] and all the "heads of the f[athers of the congre]gation with the wise [ones of the

[2] Because of a trivial error in copying, the scribe has repeated the end of this passage twice.

[3] Formula borrowed from *Num.* 16:2. It is used again two lines below, and again in the *War Scroll*, II:6-7.

[4] Allegro makes use of this term, which he translates as *beget*, to conclude that "it is not impossible that we have in this phrase a contributory factor to the Church's conception of 'the only-begotten of the Father' " (*The Dead Sea Scrolls*, p. 152). But: 1) The editor states that one of the letters of the word translated *brings to birth* is doubtful, and then we might perhaps have the passive *is born.* 2) The presence of the word as restored in the passage is no more than arguable conjecture, for it is a little short (four letters and two spaces) for the size of the lacuna. In the line above, a lacuna only two millimeters longer is filled with seven letters and two spaces. 3) The manifest meaning of the passage is: "If God wishes that the Anointed one live in those days," and not: "If God begets the Anointed one among them." 4) The Old Testament also uses this term with *God* as subject (*Isa.* 66:9), and in this case there is no doubt that it means *cause to be born* and not *beget.*

Dr. Yadin proposes an entirely different reading of this passage: "On the occasion of their meeting, [the] anointed [priest] will come with them [and shall regis]ter the whole congregation of Israel . . ." (*Journal of Biblical Literature*, September, 1959, p. 238–41).

[5] The plural sign has been omitted in the transcription, but it is clearly visible in the photograph of the manuscript.

[6] An allusion to the regulations set forth in *Num.* Chap. 2 and 10, concerning the installation of the camps and the order of march.

holy congregation][7] shall sit down before them, each in proportion to his dignity and [if] they join toge[ther for a] common [ta]ble [or to drink the w]ine and [let] the common table [be] prepared [and the] wine [poured] for drinking, [no] one [shall stretch forth] his hand towards the first portion of bread and [of wine] before the priest, for [it is for him to] bless the first portions of bread and of win[e and to extend] his hand first towards the bread; th[en] shall the Anointed of Israel ext[end] his hands towards the bread [and then] shall all [the members of] the congregation of the Community give bles[sing], each in proportion to his dignity. According to this rule shall it be done at every me[al where] so many as ten m[en be gathered toge]ther (*Rule for the Whole Congregation of Israel*, II:11-22).[8]

They labor with great diligence till the fifth hour. After which they assemble themselves together again into one place, and when they have clothed themselves in white veils, they then bathe their bodies in cold water. And after this purification is over, they every one meet together in an apartment of their own, into which it is not permitted to any of another sect to enter; while they go, after a pure manner, into the dining room, as into a certain holy temple, and quietly set themselves down; upon which the baker lays them loaves in order; the cook also brings a single plate of one sort of food, and sets it before every one of them; but a priest says grace before meat, and it is unlawful for any one to taste of the food before grace be said. The same priest, when he hath dined, says grace after meat, and when they begin, and when they end, they praise God, as he that bestows their food upon them; after which they lay aside their (white) garments, and betake themselves to their labors again till the evening; then they return home to supper, after the same manner, and if there be any strangers there, they sit down with them (Josephus, *Jewish Wars*, II, VIII, 5; 129-32).

[7] Another formula borrowed from *Num.* 31:26, and used similarly in the *War Scroll*, II:1, 3, 7; III:4.
[8] *Qumran Cave I*, No. 28 a, pp. 110–11. (The restorations adopted are those of the editor, Père Barthélemy.)

[The Essenes] choose certain stewards . . . such as are good men and priests; who are to get their corn and their food ready for them (Josephus, *Antiquities of the Jews*, XVIII, I, 5,22).

These, then, are the texts on which Dupont-Sommer bases his statement that,

Amongst the Essenes the meals were taken in common and were essentially sacred meals. Here then are priests who . . . have become principally ministers of the Communion, the most important liturgical act of the sect (*The Dead Sea Scrolls; a Preliminary Survey*, p. 90). In the Christian Church, just as in the Essene Church, the essential rite is the sacred meal, whose ministers are the priests (*Ibid.*, p. 99).

Starting from the same base, other authors have gone even farther. A. Powell Davies quite confidently fills in the missing details:

It seems altogether likely, therefore, that the bread represented the Messiahs of Aaron and of Israel in the Sacramental meal of Qumran covenanters. . . . For our covenanters at Qumran, (the wine) was the blood—the life—of the Messiahs. Through the bread that was flesh and the wine that was blood the Messiahs were present with their people. Through the bread that was broken and eaten, and the cup that was passed from one to another, the Messiahs entered into the very life itself of their communicants and all were as one, mystically united. This, then, was the Essenic sacred meal, so close as to be almost identical with the sacred meal of the early Christians (*The Meaning of the Dead Sea Scrolls*, pp. 100-101).

But now, let us reread the texts themselves. What do we find?
—That the Essenes, ever obsessed with legal purity, cleansed themselves before meals with special ablutions;

but all Jews did the same (*Mark*, 7:3-4; text cited p. 87); and the Essenes went so far as to purify themselves during *three days* before their deliberative assemblies (*Rule for the Whole Congregation of Israel*, 1:26).

—That they donned special garments, reserved for the purpose; but it was the only way to avoid the risk of contracting a new defilement,[9] if the clothes had themselves touched some contaminated object; and they were not alone in practising this ceremonial. Jesus assumes it in the parable of the guests invited at the last moment (*Matt.* 22:11-12).

—That they were ranked in a strict hierarchical order, precedence being given the priests; but this was usual in all their assemblies (see the *Rule of the Community*, II:19-23, and the *Damascus Document*, XIII:2; XIV:3-6) and we know from the Gospel that such regulations were not unnecessary (*Luke* 14:7-11).

—That they ate frugally, of bread and wine with only one additional dish at each meal, as was required by their ideal of poverty and equality.[10]

—That the preparation of food and drink was reserved for the priests, probably to guarantee as far as possible against legal impurities.[11]

[9] It was precisely in order to avoid the slightest risk of legal impurity for the brotherhood that novices (*Rule of the Community*, VI:20–21) and those being punished (*Ibid.*, VII:19–20) might not participate in the communal meal until after their admission to the "baths of purification."

[10] In truth, the main stuff of every meal was, and remained, according to ancient Jewish belief, bread—to the point that the expression "break bread" was the natural synonym for "take a meal" or "eat." The *Halaka* also knew this usage. It specifies that, "if bread and something else be eaten, the benediction is pronounced only over the bread" (Strack-Billerbeck, *op. cit.*, IV:2, pp. 613–14).

[11] Nevertheless, in the *War Scroll*, VIII, 3, the "preparer(s) of the provisions" seem to be neither priests nor levites.

—That a benediction preceded the meal and another prayer followed it, according to a practice entirely usual in Judaism (Strack-Billerbeck, *op. cit.*, IV, 2, pp. 627-34).

That these Essene meals display a real affinity of "style" with our present monastic meals is an obvious fact.[12] But what resemblances can we find between these and the Last Supper celebrated by Jesus on the night before His passion, to institute a "memorial" of His death and to perpetuate the presence of His body and blood through bread and wine? Since the Communion was instituted at a meal, and even a paschal meal, we naturally find there those usages common to all Jewish meals, and especially to the Passover; and in these it resembles the meals of the Essenes and those of all pious Jews. But the particular characteristics that are essential to the Last Supper, with the institution of the Eucharist, have no equivalent in the literature of Qumran, any more than they have in any other writings of Judaism.

In order to point up the difference, let us return now to the recital of the central act that gives the Last Supper all its importance.

And as they were eating, Jesus took bread, and blessed it, and broke it, and gave it to the disciples, and said, "Take, eat; this is My body,"[13] and He took the cup, and gave thanks, and gave it to them, saying, "Drink ye all of it; for this is My blood [the blood] of the New Testament,[14] which is shed for many for the remission of sins" (*Matt.* 26:26-28).

Certainly, the expression *New Testament* (or *New Cov-*

---

[12] J. van der Ploeg, O.P., has made a comprehensive study of these Essene meals in the *Journal of Semitic Studies*, No. 2, 1957, pp. 163–75.

[13] Luke adds, "which is given for you; do this in memory of me."

[14] The adjective "new" is not certain in the text of *Matthew* and *Mark*, but it is in *Luke*.

enant), which is of Biblical origin (*Jer.* 31:31), is found at Qumran, as we shall see on pp. 101-02; certainly, too, Jesus employed bread and wine, and the Essenes also ate bread and drank wine—or rather, grape juice. But these likenesses are not the essential characteristics. Rather, the essential characteristic is the memorial of the death of Jesus, it is the presence of His body in bread and His blood in wine; and this is not found at Qumran—unless we begin to suppose, with Powell Davies, that the Essenes identified the "Messiahs" with the bread and the wine! But where does he find the slightest evidence for such an identification?

Accordingly, we cannot conclude this discussion better than by listening to the words of a Jewish scholar, in his review of Dupont-Sommer's *Dead Sea Scrolls; a Preliminary Survey:*

It is nevertheless permitted us to remark that our learned brother does not always escape the temptation, perhaps insurmountable, of maximizing the importance and the singularity of the texts which are the objects of his research. And we believe also that a more direct and more intimate knowledge of the rabbinic sources, which it would be ill grace to reproach him for lacking, would have, in some cases, kept in view the particular characteristics of facts common enough in talmudic Judaism: benediction before the meal over the bread and the water, prayers night and morning where are evoked in lyric terms "the daily circuit of light and darkness," various terms to designate the heavens, the nocturnal study of the Law, all themes familiar in non-sectarian Judaism" (G. Vajda, *Revue des Etudes Juives*, 1954, p. 67).

To sum up, this examination of customary behavior gives us a somewhat qualified result: on certain points, the resemblances suggest a certain amount of imitation of Essene practices; on other points we can find only vague similarities without demonstrative value; and finally, on still other points, Christ seems to have intended to protest strongly against customs honored among the Essenes.

3. Doctrine

In dealing with doctrines, as with customs, comparison between Essenism and Christianity cannot and ought not to deal with any other data than those specific elements that are distinguishable from the traditional Biblical commandments and from the elaborations received from the diverse currents of Judaism. Thus, profound adoration of the majesty of God, respect for His omnipotence, confidence in His mercy, and submission to His laws were equally fundamental among the Essenes, among other Jews, and among Christians. The inspiration of the Scriptures, and the cult of the angels were not Essene specialties, since the Pharisees professed the same beliefs to the same degree. To develop such parallelisms would be to falsify the scientific method of comparison. But other points are more revealing by the positive or negative contacts that they manifest.

a) GRACE AND PREDESTINATION

Josephus tells us that the Essenes were differentiated from other sects because they "had a belief of leaving everything in the hands of God" (*Antiquities of the Jews,* XVIII, 1, 5, 18). The scrolls show that they had developed, even more than is found in the Old Testament, a doctrine of grace which credited God with all the good achieved by man.

To Thee, God of all knowledge, (quotation from *I Sam.* 2:3) all the works of justice and the counsel of truth; but to the sons of man the practice of iniquity and the works of wickedness (*Hymns*, I:26-27).

It is also the action of God which purifies the soul from the stain of sin which is inherent to it.

I have known that there was hope for him whom Thou hast formed from the dust for the eternal council and Thou hast purified the perverse spirit of a sinful multitude to establish them in the ranks of the army of the saints and to enter into community with the congregation of the sons of the Heavens (= the Essenes) (*Hymns*, III:20-22).

These formularies, and many another similar one, have an authentic Christian ring, and the influence attributed to the spirit of God[1] agrees equally with the thought of St. Paul (for example, *Rom.* 8:2-27).

Although the Essenes, like other Jews, would have admitted pardon for sins and the conversion of sinners, they so minimized the freedom of man before the omnipotence of God that they arrived in practice at a rigid dualism: between the "party" of right and the "party" of wrong—the Children of Light and the Children of Darkness—no compromise was possible. It was God Himself who had fixed the destiny of men in one camp or the other.

According as a man shall have for his heritage truth and justice, he will hate perversity; but according to his adherence to perversity and unbelief, he will detest the right (*Rule of the Community*, IV, 24-25).

. . . This opposition and this contest between good and evil is also found up to a certain point in the New Testament, especially in the Gospel of St. John; but there the

[1] See the texts cited on pp. 37–42.

constitution of the two camps results from the exercise of personal freedom.

And this is the judgment, that the light has come into the world, and men loved darkness rather than light, because their deeds were evil. For every one who does evil hates the light, and does not come to the light, lest his deeds should be exposed. But he who does what is true comes to the light, that it may be clearly seen that his deeds have been wrought in God (*John* 3:19-21).

Furthermore, the Essenes considered this division of mankind as already accomplished finally, whereas for Christians it was only at the Judgment Seat that the destiny of each man would be fixed in irrevocable fashion. We recall the allegories of the tares (*Matt.* 13:24-30 and 37-43), and the fishes (*Matt.* 13:47-50), as well as the description of the Last Judgment (*Matt.* 25:31-46). In spite of this, the Essene dualism may well be reflected to some degree in Christian thought.

b) MESSIANIC EXPECTATION

The Qumran texts agree in expecting the presence of two *Messiahs*,[2] one of Aaron and one of Israel; and in this they were opposed to the whole of Biblical tradition, continued in Judaism and in Christianity. Perhaps the Essenes had arrived at this strange conception under the influence of *Zachariah* 4:14, which places next to the Lord of all the earth "two sons by oil"—that is to say, two consecrated ones. Perhaps they simply wished to emphasize that the high priest, having himself also received a special unction, was a consecrated being, even as the future liberator of the people would be. Perhaps they were trying above all to maintain the prerogatives of the

[2] See the texts cited on pp. 19 ff.

priesthood and to avoid having a priest placed lower than a "layman": for precedence in the refectory they were very careful to place the "Messiah of Israel" after all the priests.[3] Whatever the case, the messianic conceptions of the Essenes were not in accord with the ideas of Christianity, since Jesus was not a priest according to the Jewish Law. Yet they may, none-the-less, have influenced certain of the Church Fathers, like Hippolytus and St. Ambrose, since these emphasized that, through His mother, Jesus belonged after all to the priestly tribe of Levi.

c) SALVATION BY FAITH

Another analogy has been noted between faith in the Teacher of Righteousness and faith in Christ. Let the texts speak for themselves:

All those who shall have persevered in these rules, to behave themselves according to the Law, who have obeyed the voice of the Teacher, who have acknowledged their sins before God . . . who have not raised a hand against his holy precepts, his righteous commandments and his true witnesses, who have conformed themselves to the first rules by which the men of the Community were governed, who shall have lent the ear to the voice of the Teacher of Righteousness, who have not answered back on hearing the holy commandments. . . . God will pardon them and they shall see His salvation (*Damascus Document*, XX:27-34).

"The just shall live by his faith" (*Hab.* 2:4). The explanation of this refers to all who practice the Law in the House of Judah, whom God will deliver from the House of Judgment because of their affliction and of their faith in the Teacher of Righteousness (*Habakkuk Commentary*, VII:1-3).[4]

The agreement of these two passages permits us to clear

[3] See the texts cited on pp. 89-92.
[4] Translation of Dupont-Sommer, already cited on p. 67.

up the ambiguity contained in expressions "faith in the Teacher of Righteousness" or "faith in Christ." Is it a question of believing in the *precepts* of a teacher or of believing in the *mystery* which is the person of this teacher? The *Damascus Document* shows us clearly that for the Essenes it was a matter of the former sense: "obey the voice," "lend the ear to the voice"; whereas for the Christians it was a matter of the second sense: to believe in the divinity of Christ, as the Gospel says expressly: "These are written that you may believe that Jesus is the Christ, the Son of God; and that believing you may have life in His name" (*John* 20:31). It is astonishing, then, that Dupont-Sommer does not make this distinction but writes:

"Essential doctrine: the Faith which saves is Faith in the Teacher of Righteousness, divine Founder of the New Covenant. It is, we know, on this same passage of *Habakkuk* II:4b that Paul, the Christian Apostle, bases his doctrine of justification by faith" (*Revue de l'Histoire des Religions*, t. 137, April-June 1950, p. 162).

True, St. Paul was to utilize the same text of Habakkuk (*Rom.* 1:17; *Gal.* 3:11; *Heb.* 10:38); but twice the context makes it clear that what is meant is faith in the person of Christ: *Rom.* I:1-7, and above all, *Gal.* 3:10-14, which opposes justification by faith to justification by the Law; while the *Damascus Document*, XX, 27-34, and the *Habakkuk Commentary*, VIII, 1-3 explicitly associate obedience to the Law with obedience to the Teacher of Righteousness. The Essenes added to the precepts of the Law those of the Teacher of Righteousness. For Christians it was not obedience to precepts which justified, but rather faith in the person of Christ. Despite a similarity of vocabulary the thought is altogether different.[5]

[5] See on this subject a research paper by W. Grundemann, in *Revue de Qumrân*, No. 6 (February, 1960): "Der Lehrer der Gerechtigkeit von Qumrân und die Frange nach der Glaubensgerechtigkeit in der Theologie des Apostels Paulus."

d) THE NEW COVENANT

To describe their religious position, the Essenes called themselves men of "the New Covenant," borrowing a formulary from *Jeremiah* 31:31. Now the same expression was employed also by the Christians to designate in all its fullness the new relation that Jesus had come to establish between God and man. This coincidence, which is perhaps more than a coincidence, shows that the two religious societies were inspired by the same ideal—to reactivate at last the pact made between God and Moses (*Exod.* 24:8), broken by the faithlessness of the people. Nevertheless, a fundamental difference distinguishes the Christian "New Covenant" from the Essene "New Covenant." For the men of Qumran, the Covenant of Moses exists forever, and it is this which they wish to restore to force. "He [God] remembering His Covenant with the first ones [the Patriarchs] caused a remnant of Israel to remain" (*Damascus Document,* I, 4-5). "God remembered His Covenant with the first ones and he raised up from Aaron seers, and from Israel sages"[6] (*Ibid.,* VI:2-3). "Such is the case of the converts of Israel (who) are spread abroad in the way of the people; because of the love of God for the first ones who [witnessed] in his favor, he loves those who followed after them, for it is to them that the Covenant of the Patriarchs belongs" (*Ibid.,* VIII:16-18).[7] "The oath of the Covenant that Moses made with Israel, the Covenant of the [return to] the Law of Moses with all (his) heart and with all (his) soul" (*Ibid.,* XV, 8-10). "[   ] with you the Covenant and with all Israel; therefore shall each one

[6] The author here refers to the Essenes, applying to them a text of *Deut.* 1:13.

[7] Translation of Dupont-Sommer, *Evidences,* No. 59, p. 23, retranslated into English by the translator of this book.

swear on (his) soul to return to the Law of Moses" (*Ibid.*, XVI, 1-2).

As opposed to this, the New Covenant of Christ is another Covenant, which is substituted for the Covenant of Moses. "Abraham had two sons, one by a slave and one by a free woman . . . these women are two covenants" (*Gal.* 4:22-24). "Christ has obtained a ministry which is as much more excellent than the old as the covenant he mediates is better" (*Heb.* 8:6). "Therefore (Jesus) is the mediator of a new covenant . . . which redeems them from the transgressions under the first covenant" (*Heb.* 9:15). Finally, even more explicitly, the author of the *Epistle to the Hebrews* quotes in full the passage in *Jeremiah* 31:31-34, concerning the New Covenant and adds: "In speaking of a new covenant he treats the first as obsolete" (8:13). Thus, although the same words are used by the Essene and the Christian writers, two fundamentally different conceptions are expressed. The former wish to restore the ancient Covenant, while Christ institutes a new one.

e) THE KINGDOM OF GOD

In the one case as in the other, this Covenant is to bring about the Kingdom of God on earth. But it is quite astonishing that an idea so fundamental in Christian thinking (it is mentioned some fifty times in the Gospel of *Matthew* alone) should hold only so restricted a place among the writings of Qumran. All in all, there has been found only one single allusion to this Reign of God, and this also in a quotation from the Old Testament: "And this shall be the kingdom of the God of Israel" (*War Scroll*, VI:6, reproducing *Obad.* 21). Instead of attaching itself to the Reign of God, Essene thought moved rather towards the triumph of His people: "To exalt . . . the domination of Israel over all flesh" (*War Scroll*, XVII:7-8). "Israel for an eternal reign" (*Ibid*, XIX:8). "He shall renew for him the Covenant of the Community to reestablish the kingdom of His people" (*Benedictions*, V: 21).[8] To be sure, such a conception was current in Judaism as well as in Essenism, but it was opposed so much the more to the message of Christ, who abandoned all dreams of political leadership (*John* 18:36) in order to advance the Kingdom of God by the rebirth of the soul (*John* 3:21). Instead of worldly supremacy, Jesus announced to Jerusalem its destruction and profanation (*Matt.* 23:37-38; 24:5-35).

For the Christian, one of the essential characteristics of this Kingdom of God is its universality. The God of the Christians "will have all men to be saved, and to come unto the knowledge of the truth," and "Christ Jesus gave Himself a ransom for all" (*I Tim.* 2:4-6). Also, the grace of God is assured for all, Jew or pagan, and the Kingdom of God will arrive through a progressive spiritual transformation of the entire world, thanks to the leaven of the Gospel (*Matt.* 13:31-33; 26:13; *Luke* 12:49). These insights had already been announced in the Old Testament, in the last chapters of *Isaiah*,[9] for example; but the Essenes, like the Jews in general, seem not to have understood the importance of these oracles. For them, the pagans were wicked beings, destined to eternal punishment, who must be exterminated from the face of the earth so that there should be none left save the "righteous," the elect people. Here is the destination of the Children of Darkness: "multitudinous scourging at the hand of the angels of perdition, eternal damnation in the passion of the fury of the God of vengeance,[10] perpetual

[8] *Qumran Cave I*, no. 28 b, p. 127.
[9] *Isa.* 45:14; 20–25; 55:1–5; 56:3–8; 59:19–21; 60:1–22; 66:18–23. See also the beginning of *Isa.* (2:1–4; 19:18–25), *Jer.* 33:9, and *Ps.* 67.
[10] Quotation from *Ps.* 94:1.

terror and everlasting shame with the ignominy of destruction in the fire of darkness. During all the times of their generations they shall be in the anguish of affliction and the sorrow of bitterness in the calamities of darkness until their extermination 'without rest nor escape' "[11] (*Rule of the Community*, IV, 12-14). Such formularies were not a display of empty threats, for the Essenes looked forward to the extermination, root and branch, of all pagans and faithless Jews, as we know from the *War Scroll*: "God has smitten the Sons of Darkness. 'His anger shall not return until'[12] they have been exterminated" (III:9). "The enemy is to be pursued in the war of God in order to destroy him by everlasting destruction" (IX:5-6).

Such aims are shocking to Christian ears, accustomed to hear love for one's enemies extolled. The Old Testament commanded brotherly love: "You shall not hate your brother in your heart . . . you shall not take vengeance or bear any grudge against the sons of your own people. You shall love your neighbor as yourself" (*Lev.* 19:17-18); but it had little to say about love for one's enemies (*Exod.* 23:24-5; *I Sam.* 24:5-8, 26:9-12; *Prov;* 25:21), and sometimes exhibited actual hatred (*Ps.* 109:6-20, 119:113, 137:9, 139:22). Judaism in general followed this pattern. It saw as one's neighbors primarily the other members of the people of God, whether by nature or adoption. It did not preach hatred of enemies, but neither did it recommend love. The Essenes, on the other hand, whilst practising an admirable charity towards "good" people, and prohibiting private vengeance, made it a duty to hate "sinners." The first article of the *Rule of the Community* orders one "to love all whom (God) has chosen and to hate all whom He has rejected" (I:3-4); "to love all the

[11] Quotation from *Esd.* 9:14, which is repeated in the *War Scroll,* I, 6; IV, 2, and XIV, 5.
[12] Reference to *Jer.* 23:20.

104

Children of Light, each according to his lot in the council of God, and to hate all the Children of Darkness, each according to his guilt in the vengeance of God" (I:9-11).

The initiation ceremony of the Covenant called above all for maledictions:

The Levites curse all the men of Belial's faction. . . "May you be accursed in all the ungodly works of your guilt! May God make a horror of you by the hand of all wreckers of vengeance! May He bring about destruction behind you by the hand of all dischargers of retribution! May you be accursed without mercy according to the darkness of your works! May you be punished in the murk of the eternal fire! God will have no mercy on you when you beseech Him, and He will give no pardon for the remission of your sins. He will lift up the countenance of His wrath for vengeance (on you) and there will be no peace for you in the mouth of all those who hold to the Fathers" (*Ibid.*, II, 4-9).

Other verses of the same sort are found elsewhere in the *Rule of the Community* (II,11-17; III, 1-6; IV,9-14; IX, 21-22), in the *Damascus Document* (II:15), and in the whole of the *War Scroll*, which is animated by such a hatred of the Children of Darkness that its aim is to accomplish their "eternal destruction" by a universal slaughter. Furthermore, Josephus had already told us that the novice was "obliged to take tremendous oaths . . . that he will always hate the wicked" (*Jewish Wars*, II, VIII, 7:139).

Now let us listen to the words of Christ: "You have heard that it was said, 'You shall love your neighbor and hate your enemy.'[13] But I say to you, Love your enemies

---

[13] The first part of this phrase comes from *Lev.* 19:18, but the second is found neither in the Old Testament nor in any writings of Judaism (known to us). Probably Jesus is here referring to the teachings of the Essenes, which he condemns absolutely.

and pray for those who persecute you, so that you may be sons of your Father Who is in Heaven; for He makes His sun rise on the evil and on the good, and sends rain on the just and on the unjust" (*Matt.* 5:43-45). And many another passage emphasizes the importance of this precept: *Matt.* 18:21-35; *Luke* 6:27-38; 9:52-56; 10:27-37. Between Essenism, which made it a duty to hate the enemies of God, and Christianity, which imitated God in His love for sinners, there was more than divergence. This was complete opposition.

f) HOLY TRINITY—INCARNATION—REDEMPTION

Furthermore, the distinctive characteristic of the mind of Christ—as opposed to the Old Testament—is the reassessment of certain fundamental truths. The three essential dogmas of the new religion are the mysteries of the Holy Trinity, the Incarnation, and the Redemption. Without these, Christianity is not possible. All comparisons dealing with other points are secondary.

Now these essential beliefs were not even thought of by the Essenes. Not a single text makes reference to any plurality of persons in the Godhead. Not a single text makes mention, in the strict sense, of a Son of God made man. Not a single text makes allusion to the salvation of the world through his redemptive death. The Essenes had never even confronted the problems of the Trinity or the Incarnation as possibilities; and if they had thought of them, they would have recoiled promptly as from a horrible blasphemy.

So far as the salvation of the world was concerned— they had faced this problem but had solved it differently, in the tradition of the Old Testament. In the first place, there was to be no salvation for the "wicked," "Thou (O God) wilt not accept ransom for the offenses of ungodliness" (*Hymns* XV, 24, referring to *Num.* 35:31-32, and *Ps.* 141:4). "(God) will not pardon, forgiving your iniquities" (*Rule of the Community*, II:8).

Secondly, for the "good," salvation would be earned:

1) By a holy life.

In the spirit of rectitude and of humility his sin will be atoned (*Ibid.*, III, 8).

2) By incorporation into the Community.

The council of the Community will be strengthened in the truth for an eternal planting, a house of holiness for Israel, a foundation of the holy of holies for Aaron, witnesses of other truth for the trial of the elect of God's good will in order to make atonement for the land and to bring upon the ungodly their recompense (*Ibid.*, VIII,V-7).

(The men of the Covenant) will be (an object) of good will in order to make atonement for the land and decree the sentence of the ungodly (*Ibid.*, VIII, 10 b).

3) By the sacrifices of the Temple.

To expiate the guilt of the transgression and the waywardness of the offense, to (obtain God's) good will for the land through the flesh of burnt offerings, the fats of sacrifice and the offering of the lips (*Ibid.*, IX, 4-5).[14]

They shall be appointed to the burnt offerings and the sacrifices, to prepare a fragrant incense for God's good pleasure, to make atonement for all His congregation (*War Scroll*, II, 5-6).

4) By the mercy of God.

I found rest in Thy kindnesses and in the multitude of Thy mercies, for Thou forgivest iniquity" (*Hymns*, IV, 36-37).

[14] See p. 83, note 12.

In the abundance of His goodness He will pardon all my iniquities (*Rule of the Community*, XI, 14).
Longsuffering is with Him, and abundance of pardon, to forgive those converted from their sin (*Damascus Document*, II, 4-5).

So we may well conclude, with this same *Damascus Document* (IV, 9-10), "according to His covenant which God established with the first ones [the patriarchs] to pardon their iniquities, so God will pardon them [the Essenes]."

Nothing in all this recalls the words of Jesus about His blood, "shed for the remission of sins" (*Matt.* 26:28), nor those of the Apostles, "There is salvation in no one else [than Christ]" (*Acts*, 4:12). Thus the comparison between the doctrine accepted by the Essenes and that of Christianity turns out to be deceptive. The essentials of Christianity are absent in Essenism. Formal oppositions appear on several points; the resemblances are rare and secondary.

Certainly, we are very far from the statement of Professor Étiemble:

Henceforth . . . we *know*[15] that the Messiah of Galilee had nothing to offer—absolutely nothing—which had not been long familiar to the believers of the New Covenant. The first Christ—he who perished under Aristobolus II—could only be copied by the second Christ . . . (Jesus) had the wisdom to copy the ideas, the moral values, the theology, the discipline of his predecessor, the first Christ of our history. Because he had the facility of adapting for his own use the essentials of what, during a century, had inspired, consoled, and delighted his poor people, he had the good fortune to preach to converts (*Temps Modernes*, January, 1951, pp. 1291-92).

[15] Italics in the text.

108

4. Literary expression

When we turn from the subject of doctrine to examine its literary expression, we find a very much closer relationship between the Essene literature and the New Testament. In fact, the *Epistle of Jude* (14) actually cites the book of *Enoch* by name.[1]

For many years a number of linguistic peculiarities (particularly in the Gospel of the Infancy[2]) have given ground for the hypothesis that certain documents used by the evangelists (*Luke* 1:1) might have been composed in Hebrew instead of Aramaic. Until recently, scholars have hesitated to accept this theory, for Hebrew was supposed to have been a dead language in the time of Christ. Now, the Qumran texts show us that at this period people were still able to write in good Hebrew. Moreover, the Essenes seem to have been, at least in part, the authors of this renaissance, for one of their reproaches against their adversaries was that these had bartered away the source of knowledge "for uncircumcised lips and the foreign speech of a people without understanding"[3] (*Hymns* II, 19). "It is with (lying) lips and foreign speech that they speak to thy people"[4] (*Ibid.*, IV, 16). Therefore, we may perhaps owe to the Essenes the choice of the Hebrew language for the first writing of the earliest Christian documents.

The poems known as *Magnificat* (*Luke* 1:46-55), *Bene-*

[1] This section is more condensed than those which precede it, for it bears on the work of Christ only in a secondary manner. Much helpful information on these points will be found in the work of Jean Daniélou, S.J., *The Dead Sea Scrolls and Primitive Christianity*.

[2] See, for example, a treatment of this subject by R. Laurentin in *Biblica*, No. 4, (1956), pp. 453-56.

[3] The author combines phrases from *Exod.* 6:12 and *Isa.* 33:19.

[4] Quotation from *Isa.* 28:11.

dictus (Luke 1:68-79), and *Nunc Dimittis* (*Luke* 2:29-32) were composed of Biblical reminiscences, according to an "anthology" technique altogether common in the *Rule of the Community*, the *War Scroll*, and the *Hymns*. Furthermore, their style is related in a characteristic way to that of the Qumran writings.

Various authors[5] have pointed out an impressive number of expressions used both at Qumran and in the synoptic Gospels (especially in the Sermon on the Mount)[6]; but we cannot draw any conclusions about a direct relation, for there are too many factors concerning the literary scene of the day of which we are ignorant.

With St. Paul the contacts are more precise. Perhaps he drew inspiration from *Hymn* X:14, "Blessed [be] thou O Lord, God of all mercies [and Father of all] grace!" when he wrote: "Blessed be God . . . the Father of mercies and the God of all comfort" (*II Cor.* 1:3). In any case, the same second epistle to the Corinthians (6-15) uses the term *Belial* to designate the chief of demons, and this usage is typically Essene.[7] In the Old Testament and the writings of Judaism the same term never has more than adjective value for describing a "wicked" being. And even certain words of the Pauline vocabulary, such as *lot* and *mystery*,[8] seem freighted with a truly Essene resonance.

[5] For example, Kuhn, "Die in Palästina gefunden hebräischen Texte und das Neue Testament," *Zeitschrift für Theologie und Kirche*, 1950, pp. 192–211; also Grossouw, "The Dead Sea Scrolls and the New Testament," *Studia Theologica*, 1951, pp. 289–99, and 1952, pp. 1–8.

[6] See Schubert, "The Sermon on the Mount and the Qumran Texts," in Krister Stendahl's collective book, *The Scrolls and the New Testament*, pp. 118–28.

[7] There is abundant evidence for this, whether from the Qumran texts (which include also part of the book of *Jubilees*), or from those works which used Essene materials, such as the *Ascension of Isaiah* and the *Testaments of the Twelve Patriarchs*.

[8] See the study by Father Ernest Vogt, S.J. " 'Mysteria' in textibus Qumran," in *Biblica*, No. 2, (1956), pp. 247–57.

Finally, the resemblances become even more numerous and revealing with St. John.[9] In his Gospel the metaphor of light and darkness, to symbolize good and evil, takes on the same value as in certain works at Qumran. In the Prologue, the creative role of the Word is expressed by a phrase that condenses a theme of the *Rule of the Community* (XI, 11; 17-18) and *Hymns* (I, 8 and X, 9); and the rest of the Gospel presents a whole sequence of "contacts in series."[10] The *Apocalypse* borrows a literary style much in favor among the Essenes, and the whole of Chapter XII, the vision of the "woman in travail," is in curious parallelism with one of the *Hymns* (III, 7-8). So many significant facts suggest that the Apostle John had a particular familiarity with the Essenes. By way of pure hypothesis, we could perhaps hazard the following guess: we know from Josephus (*Life*, 10-11) that some young men made a sort of progression through the various religious groups before fixing their choice on one of them, and we know from the Evangelist himself that he had some relation with the High Priest, chief of the Sadducee party (*John* 18:15). In this case, we can easily imagine that a soul so profoundly inspired by God would have sought from childhood to join himself to each of the religious movements of his time; but finding nowhere a reality worthy of his ideal, he would have passed successively from the Essenes to the Sadducees, and perhaps also to the Pharisees, whom he combats in his Gospel with a

[9] See in particular the stimulating article by Rev. J. M. Braun, "'L'arrière fond judaïque du quatrième évangile et la Communauté de l'Alliance," *Revue Biblique*, No. 1, 1955, pp. 5–44. See also Father R. E. Brown, "The Qumran Scrolls and the Johannine Gospel and Epistles," in Krister Stendahl's collective book, *The Scrolls and the New Testament*, pp. 183–204; and the same author's "The Semitic Background of the New Testament Mysterion," in *Biblica*, No. 4, (1958), pp. 426–48, and No. 1, (1959), pp. 70–84.

[10] Father Braun in the article cited above.

particular insistence, as if he had retained an especially unhappy memory of them, before following John the Baptist, and then leaving him to give his allegiance finally to Jesus. From his period of Essene "postulancy" he would have carried away a literary orientation; and it may also have been here that he discovered the virtue of chastity, since tradition presents him as the virgin Apostle.

Whatever the truth of this hypothesis, which is of minor importance in any case, the Essene works allow us to see and appreciate one of the factors that influenced, more or less profoundly according to the authors, the composition of the New Testament.

If we try to bring together the many factors in this comparative study, we find that the resulting picture is very complex. Christ had almost no distinctive doctrine in common with His so-called predecessor, in spite of having, like him, gathered disciples and suffered persecutions (but of what religious leader could not the same be said?). Nevertheless, on numerous points of detail He readily adapted Himself to His times, and thus profited by the useful example of the Essenes to borrow this or that of their practices. On the doctrinal level He could hardly have met with these stern partisans of the Mosaic Law; so he would have left them to their intransigence and given Himself to His proper task—which was to found His church, to reveal the mysteries of the divine life, to teach the world that God is love (1 John 4:8), and then to give His life as a ransom for many (Matt. 20:28). But in His words He may have made allusion to various writings known to His auditors, and in any case, His disciples delved readily enough in these treasures to enrich their own expositions.

To put it differently, if the Essenes had not existed, the life of Christ would have been in no wise affected in its general pattern, but this or that particular detail might have been altered. Christian doctrine would have presented at least the same fundamental aspects, but its literary expression might have been different in several respects.

IV

The Teacher of
Righteousness Self-Revealed

U P TO this point, the comparison we have made between the Teacher of Righteousness and Christ has
been based on texts which tell us, explicitly or implicitly,
about the Teacher. But we possess also a number of
poems in which the author speaks to us in his own person
and in terms that call vividly to mind the personality of
the Teacher of Righteousness himself. It is true that this
identification is not universally accepted. Bardtke considers it "gratuitous" and "premature," while Burrows and
Gaster remain sceptical. Nevertheless, it is sufficiently
reasonable to have gained a number of votes already and
to deserve being taken into consideration.

The author of these poems appears in the role of head
and founder of "his" community. We must look for him,
therefore, among the several "superiors" who presided
over the destinies of the Essenes (or rather over one of the
Essene groups, if this wording be preferred). Furthermore, he had been the victim of furious persecution and he
possessed a literary talent and a religious perception of the
first order. Now the Teacher of Righteousness, so far as
our knowledge goes, is the only Essene who had been
subjected to such opposition, and who had exercised so
profound an influence on the souls of his disciples.

If we accept this attribution, these poems become the best of evidence concerning the intimate life of the Teacher, and thus should be a basis for any valid comparison between him and Jesus. The biographical information is too scanty for our liking, but these lyrical outpourings reveal to us, with moving sincerity, the meditations of a soul drawn always towards God.

If we read through these precious poems thoughtfully, remembering the Oriental taste for colorful imagery, the Semitic fondness for well-balanced repetitions, and the Essene taste for numerous Biblical references, a self-portrait of the Teacher will be seen to emerge.*

Only a single allusion carries us back to the far distant time when his vocation was decided: when he swore an oath upon his soul "to commit no sin" against his God, "to do no wrong before (His) eyes," and so was led to the community of "the men of my fellowship."

That he had known violence and suffering there can be no doubt. With great emphasis he recalls having been held in captivity, where he ate "sighing as (his) bread," and his drink (was) "mingled with endless tears." These afflictions "ate into his very bones, shaking his spirit and crushing his strength"; and he was brought to the bitter realization that the powers of evil could transform the very works of God into something shameful.

We cannot doubt that this captivity was savage in its cruelty. He speaks of the feel of irons—of unbreakable cords and fetters unshatterable—a prison barred with iron and with doors of bronze. Such was the physical suffering of this period that his heart "poured forth like water," his "flesh melted like wax," his "knees became as water," and

* The following pages have been abridged by the translator, retaining the explanatory comments of the author. The complete text, with identification of all Biblical references, will be found on pp. 133–158.

he quotes from the lamentations of Job. Yet, in reflecting on this phase of his life, his greatest regret appears to be that he was denied the opportunity of helping others—that he found himself mute at a time when he knew that the Lord had given him a life-saving message.

Next, the Teacher complains of having been exiled—driven as a bird from its nest to a far country, where his companions and friends thought of him as of one who is dead. His place of sojourn is not named, but he seems to make allusion to the banks of the Nile in a vivid picture of hunting and fishing in this country—hunting beasts destined to meet condemned criminals in the arena, "lions that break all the bones of the mighty and drink the blood of the brave"; and the more peaceful occupation of the fishermen "spreading their nets on the face of the waters."

The Teacher's thoughts often turn to his enemies, but a special bitterness colors the memory of certain disciples who turned traitor. Those who had eaten his bread, "lifted their heel against (him) and slandered (him) with a perverse tongue—even the associates of (his) fellowship." God had ordained the way of holiness for them, but they had strayed from that way and were "taken captive by their own lust."

And even more serious than their own condemnation, in his eyes, was the fact that they had perverted others by their offenses. They pushed back into the Pit the life of the man who had been taught God's doctrine, and they bartered away wisdom and truth for the "uncircumcized lips and the foreign speech of a people without understanding, in order to lead them to ruin."

There is a quality of ironical disillusionment in his reflections on the contradictory role in which he had served—a symbol of inspiration to some souls, and an object of hatred to others: "a snare to wrongdoers and a source of healing to those who turn from transgressions";

117

a man of contention for the interpreters of wrong, but a peace-maker to those who saw the truth.

His sufferings are described in a series of graphic images —he was like a sailor amidst the raging of the seas, with billows roaring over him; it was like the convulsions of a woman in travail; the waves of death and of Sheol rolled over the bed of his slumbers. But always he was marvelously sustained and delivered by God, to whom he offers all his gratitude:

I give thee thanks, O my Lord . . .
Thou hast delivered the life of the needy
Whose blood they were preparing to waste,
Pouring it out because of thy service.
Thou, O my God, hast assisted the soul of the afflicted and the destitute . . .
And hast redeemed my soul from the hands of the mighty.

In his own view, the providential reason for the trials that beset him was precisely that God might be furnished the occasion for glorifying Himself in the deliverance of the righteous and the punishment of the wicked:

Only according to thy will have they led their assault against my life,
That thou mightest be glorified in the judgment of the ungodly,
And mightest be magnified in me before the children of men;
For by thy favor do I stand upright.

The sense of profound gratitude to the Almighty, which has given the name of the *Thanksgiving Hymns* to these poems, runs through them like a continuous obbligato. The Lord closed the mouth of the lions' whelps and placed a muzzle over their teeth; he provided refuge in the sight of the sons of men. In order to magnify Himself, He acted wondrously toward the needy:

118

Thou hast put him into the furnace like gold tried by fire,
Like silver molten in a crucible . . .
But thou, O my God, madest the storm be still
And didst deliver the soul of the needy.

In short, the Teacher emerged victorious from these trials, and they contributed to the radiance of his spirit. God had "exalted his horn over all his detractors" and, like Isaiah, he had "appeared in the sevenfold light." In the glory of the Lord his own light found its source and out of the darkness God made the light to shine.

Nor would he stand alone in this vindication from on High. His enemies were to be punished, but his disciples were to partake of his triumph and assist in the destruction of the ungodly. His God-inspired mission was to make a division between the wicked and the righteous. Those who had opposed him would be put to shame.

I shall arise and stand upright before them that deride me,
My hand above all my scorners. . . .

But for those who listened to him, who walked in the way of God's heart, who volunteered for service in the company of the saints and joined together in the Lord's Covenant, the greatest rewards were reserved. They were the remnant of God's people, preserved by grace from their enemies and refined so that they might be pure of all offence; and they would destroy all the peoples of other lands and execute judgment on all transgressors of God's commandments.

For the Teacher was conscious of fulfilling a providential mission and accomplishing a wonderful work. Through him illumination had been given to many. His personal apprehension of the marvel of God's secret counsel had become through him a marvel known to persons too many

119

to number; and it had been his privilege to make known to the sons of men the mighty deeds of God.

> Thou hast made fast on the rock my house
> And the eternal foundations of my fellowship;
> All my walls form a rampart, proven and unshakable.

In a touching passage he describes the vocation of the Teacher, who "makes a shoot grow up" and preserves its strength. And again, he sees himself as a "father" whom God has given to the children of grace;

> And like a guardian to men of good omen.
> They opened their mouth like the nursling
> And like the sucking child in the bosom of its nurse.

To describe the beneficial results of his teaching he turns to the Biblical image of an oasis surrounding a spring. God has placed in his mouth as it were a freshet of the autumn rain and a spring of living water for the thirsty ground. Here there has grown up a well-watered garden,

A planting of pines, of planes
And also of cypress, brought together for thy glory . . .

On the shoot grown beside this fountain shall all the beasts of the forest feed;
The garden about its stem shall be for all who pass along the way,
And its branches for every winged bird.

Yet the Teacher never lets himself fall victim to pride, and he is always conscious of the wretchedness of the human condition. For him, man is a creature "modelled of clay and kneaded with water," conceived in degradation and born tainted with sin, "perverted, without understanding, and terrified by the judgments of Righteousness." Of himself he is nothing.

What shall I say that is not known?
And what shall I proclaim that has not been told?

I, who am but dust and ashes—
What can I plan, unless thou hast willed it,
And what can I decide, apart from thy good pleasure?
With what can I arm myself, unless thou sustainest me,
And how can I have wisdom, unless thou hast formed it in me?
What can I preach, unless thou hast opened my mouth,
And how can I answer, unless thou givest me wisdom?

The Teacher is willing to admit himself a sinner, albeit one who has been purified through divine mercy. Insofar as he belongs to ungodly humanity, to the carnal fellowship of unrighteousness, his iniquities, his faults, his sins, together with the "perversity of his heart"—all these things relate him to "the vermin that crawl in darkness." He acknowledges his own guilt and the faithlessness of his forefathers; and he realizes that of himself he has no claim on God.

Because of my sins I am forsaken, outside thy covenant.

But he understands also the beauty of forgiveness for the penitent soul.

For I have recognized thy truth;
I have assented to my sentence,
And I have accepted my ordeal . . .

I have delighted in thy pardons
As if they consoled me for the original fault.
I have known that there is hope in thy kindnesses
And confidence in the abundance of thy strength.

121

In God, furthermore, the Teacher finds the source of all the favors with which he has been showered. Whatever righteousness he has, whatever uprightness of heart, whatever perfection of his way—all these come from the Lord. His own illumination is from the wellspring of divine wisdom; and in contemplation of the marvellous works of God, his heart has seen the future revealed.

For God's truth is the rock of my footsteps;
His might, the support of my right hand,
And from the wellspring of his righteousness (comes) my
    justification.
The light in my heart (comes) from his marvellous secrets,
My eye has beheld the eternal Being:
Skill which is concealed from man to know,
Knowledge of proficiency beyond the (reach of) carnal
    humankind.

To those whom God has chosen,
He has given an eternal possession,
He has granted (them) the portion of the saints.
With the sons of Heaven he has joined their fellowship,
For the counsel of the Community, the foundation of the Holy
    building,
The eternal planting enduring through all ages to come . . .

For his way (belongs) not to man (himself),
(And it is) not (in) man to direct his steps.
For to God (belongs) the verdict,
And from his hand (comes) the perfection of conduct.
By his wisdom all things have (their) existence.
He established everything there is in accordance with his plan,
And without him was not anything made.

The Teacher's greatest desire was to consecrate himself wholly to the praise and glory of the divine Majesty—"to lift up the flute of his lips to the measure of God's decree."

With the coming of day and night
I would enter into the covenant of God;
With the going of evening and morning
I shall recite his commandments . . .

To God I say: O, my Righteousness!
And to the Most High: O, thou Source of all my Good!
Wellspring of Wisdom, Fountain of Holiness,
Height of Glory, Almighty of Eternal Splendor;
I would choose that which he teaches me;
I would love that which he awards.
Whenever I put forth hand or foot
I shall bless his name.
Whenever I go out or come in—
When I sit down or stand up—
Or when I lay me down on my bed—
I shall exult in him and shall bless him,
(With) the offering issuing from my lips,
For the table spread before men—
Before I lift my hands
To nourish myself with the delights of the produce of earth—
In the moment of fright and terror—
In the place of agony and desolation—
I shall bless him in his increasing marvels,
And shall glorify his might.
By his mercies, I shall be supported all the day long,
And I shall know that the judgment of all things living is in
   his hand,
And that all his works (are) truth.
At the beginning of agony I shall laud him,
And at deliverance I shall exult again.

Finally, the fervor of his piety leads the Teacher, out of
the inspiration of the Old Testament, to discover in God
the most beautiful of all titles—that of "Father":

For thou, more than my father, hast understood me;
More than my mother hast thou cared for me . . .

From my youth upward thou hast appeared to me in the
  wisdom of thy judgment,
In steadfast truth thou hast sustained me,
In thy spirit of holiness thou delightest me.

For my father did not understand me
And my mother has abandoned me to thee.
But thou art a father to all the children of truth,
And thou hast rejoiced over them as a mother over her babe;
And as one who carries the sucking child in his bosom,
So dost thou encompass thy creation.

Reading these poems, we cannot but feel intense admiration for their author. The spirit that burned with such
a spiritual flame must be ranked among the noblest figures
of the Old Testament. Like the prophets and the psalmists,
he was lifted up into the very presence of God. He contemplated His greatness, His wisdom, His might, His
mercy—and his soul was afire with sincere love of the
divine Majesty. He braved violent opposition and no suffering could shake his confidence in God or his devotion
to His service. He stands before us in the nobility of a
soul truly "seduced" by God.

The Biblical reminiscences which pour forth incessantly
in his psalms are indication enough of the source of his
spiritual life. Actually, he invented nothing; and his glory
is not primarily in having enriched the religious patrimony
of his people. Rather, he assimilated and mirrored in a
wonderful way the riches the Old Testament bestowed on
him, and it is his incontestable glory that he was one of
the most beautiful flowers to have bloomed in the garden
of Jewish revelation.

Nevertheless, all our legitimate admiration does not
make him comparable to Jesus, nor especially does it cause
us to see in him the model copied by Christ. Between

these two a great difference shines forth, just as it does between Jesus and all the greatest heroes and saints.

The Teacher restricted the paternity of God to the "children of truth" and was very careful not to extend it to sinners. The insistence with which he recalled his tribulations shows how deeply he had been hurt by his ordeal. He never speaks a word of pardon, but rather pursues his enemies with the threat of inexorable divine punishments. In his sufferings he recognized a means of exalting divine might; but he never realized the value of love, or of expiation, which embodies the very offering of suffering itself. With absolute honesty he recognized himself a sinner, infected by the weaknesses common to human nature, and never dared to pretend to any participation in the divine nature. His vocation was that of a religious leader who sets forth the ideas by which he is imbued and who inspires the disciples assembled about him; but he never contemplated presenting himself as the savior of the world. No more did he dream of applying to himself any particular messianic reference, and he proclaimed only that the men of his community would one day accomplish the judgment of God by the extermination of the ungodly. Above all, he had no special revelation concerning such fundamental mysteries as the Holy Trinity, the Incarnation, and the Redemption.

In brief, all that is inherent in the personality and the message of Christ—all that distinguishes Him specifically from the other holy persons of the Old Testament—all this is entirely lacking in the Teacher of Righteousness, a rival of the great prophets.

Conclusion

This detailed comparison of the Teacher of Righteousness with Christ has allowed us to record, as we went along, the invaluable results of the discoveries at Qumran.

We have admired the peak of holiness a noble soul could reach, when guided and inspired by the assiduous reading of the Old Testament.

We have gathered new information about the trends of thought common to the minds of people at the time of Christ's coming; and thus, as Dupont-Sommer truly observed, "Jesus and the nascent Christian Church will find themselves more firmly rooted in history" (*The Dead Sea Scrolls; a Preliminary Survey*, p. 100).

We have come to know works that may have been in the hands of many hearers of Christ, and thus we can better identify in the apostolic teachings what conforms to these surrounding ideals, what is reaction against abuses and distortions, what is outright condemnation of outdated practices and erroneous ideas, and what is a new and personal deposit due to a positive revelation.

We have discovered, as between these works and the New Testament, various literary affinities that cannot be explained if their dates of composition were very far apart. It is true that in any epoch it is possible to imitate earlier writings; but, in this case there is no question of imitation, even if unconscious. Rather, we see spontaneous expressions of the same psychological context. It will not be possible in future, without flying in the face of all probability, to assign any passage of the New Testament to a second century date.

We have observed that the conduct of Christ and his disciples resembled certain Essene usages. But this gives us good reason for believing that the Gospel accounts preserve a faithful picture of the reality, whether they were composed before the destruction of Essenism between 66 and 70 A.D., or whether, if composed later, they were based on earlier documents or the reproduction of an unaltered tradition.

We have noted that among these parallel practices it is the organization of the two communities, Christian and Essene, which provides the chief similarities. Therefore it can no longer be considered unlikely that Christ intended to found a visible and hierarchical society. Quite the opposite is probable, and the example of the Essenes would have encouraged Jesus to plan, for his disciples, a religious movement similarly structured and equally as vigorous as Essenism, even though it were animated by the most complete universality.

Finally, we have established that the doctrine of Christ diverged from that of Essenism even more than from that of Phariseeism. This radical opposition can hardly result from a spontaneous evolution produced by any "collective mentality." It requires, initially, a strong personality reacting powerfully against the normal tendencies of His time. Thus the historic reality of Christ's life is not only confirmed but is seen to be a necessary prerequisite for the development of Christian doctrine. To see in His person and His life only the product of a "myth" requires as a preliminary assumption the existence of a tendency towards Christianity seeking to crystallize itself in the Hebrew community. But the more we learn of the Jewish *milieu* of those times, the more are we obliged to recognize that it moved naturally toward either the restrictions of Phariseeism or the extremes of Essenism. In such an atmosphere, if Christ had not lived, Christianity could never have been born.[1]

So far as similarities between Christ and the Teacher of Righteousness are concerned, we can now understand the deeper meaning and importance of the positions discussed at the beginning of this study.

A journalist conjures up a new round in the eternal bout between science and religion, reason and faith: Michel Pontleroy, in *Fémina-Illustration*, September 1956, p. 45. True enough: if it be assumed in advance that science is always opposed to religion and reason to faith, then these scientific discoveries *must* furnish a new argument to confound religion and faith.

Without definitely expressing such a doctrine, some people nevertheless tend to reduce religious history to the level of social history. For them religion *cannot* be revealed by God. It is no more than a result of natural evolution. Therefore Christianity must be explained by historical factors, and so in part by Essenism.

On the other hand, some apologists have at times minimized the value of science; and the Christian scholar should guard carefully against the danger of letting the ardor of his faith dim the clarity of his critical sense. The religious mind would be seriously compromised in advance if it were denied a part in the stimulating debate over scientific truth.

[1] Dupont-Sommer is in substantial accord with this conclusion: "The appearance of faith in Jesus—the foundation of the New Church—can scarcely be explained without the real, historical activity of a new Prophet, a new Messiah, who rekindled the flame and concentrated on himself the adoration of men" (*The Dead Sea Scrolls; a Preliminary Survey*, pp. 99-100). If the adjective "new" and the prefix of "rekindled" were omitted this statement would be eminently satisfactory.

But the barrier between these opposing tendencies is not insurmountable, and we can hope that believers and nonbelievers alike will find common ground in method. In the problem with which we are concerned, the argument will be greatly clarified if both sides will agree, cost what it may, to respect the following principles:

Consider *all* the texts, and *nothing but* the texts.

Consider as proofworthy only those texts whose readings and translations are indisputable, and allow for a certain margin of error in texts whose interpretation remains uncertain.

When a relation is found between a Qumran text and a Christian one, begin by finding out if the dependence is real; for we cannot identify any certain influence of one on the other if the same *motif* is found also in the Old Testament or the writings of Judaism.

Make an honest total of the resemblances *and* the differences, first on points considered of major importance by Essenes or Christians, and then on points considered secondary by one or the other.

And then scholars, whether or not they are believers, will surely agree on the following conclusions:

1) No text speaks unequivocally of the incarnation, messiahship, divinity, crucifixion, or return in glory of the Teacher of Righteousness.

2) Several Christian texts show a *literary* influence from the Essene texts; and certain practices of Christ and the first Christians imitate those of the Essenes. But these derivations concern only secondary points and their percentage is negligible as compared with the numerous divergencies affecting essential points.

3) The comparison ought above all to bear on the *doctrinal elements,* and here we can list almost nothing but oppositions, especially as they bear on

the more fundamental beliefs. And among the various Jewish sects of the day, Essenism departs farthest from the direction taken by Christianity.

Surely, we can never honor sufficiently the astonishing figure of the Teacher of Righteousness. His piety and courage constitute a magnificent example for any age. His poems, directly or indirectly, must have touched many hearts by the sincerity and intensity of his religious experience. The renaissance of the spiritual life which he encouraged probably prepared many souls to receive the Christian message. On several minute points his influence inspired certain of the words or actions of Christ.

It would, however, be a distortion of historic reality if we tried, beyond and against the evidence of the texts actually known, to make of him an *"Essene Messiah,"* a *"Christ ante litteram,"* the *model copied by Jesus of Nazareth.* He was a spiritual director; but he was in no way—and he never represented himself as being—*"the Savior of the World."*

We have in addition the formal testimony of those who knew him best and loved him most. To describe the personality and work of their revered master, the Essenes chose only the phrase *"Teacher of Righteousness."* The disciples of Jesus, on the contrary, recognized in Him *"The Christ, the Son of the Living God"* (*Matt.* 16:16) and *"The Word made Flesh"* (*John* 1:14). The difference in these formulas corresponds exactly to the difference in the reality.

Texts from the
Qumran Hymns

COMPLETE TEXT OF ALL THE HYMNS
OF QUMRAN WHICH APPEAR TO BE
AUTOBIOGRAPHICAL AND TO SUGGEST
THE PERSONALITY OF THE TEACHER
OF RIGHTEOUSNESS

*Translated from
the Hebrew into French by*
JEAN CARMIGNAC

and rendered into English by
KATHARINE G. PEDLEY

IN 1961 THE author published a complete translation of all the *Hymns* found in Cave I, with extensive notes and an introductory essay dealing with the text itself and the rules of prosody as practised at Qumran (*Les Textes de Qumran*, Letouzey et Ané, Paris, 1961, pp. [127]-282). The present selection consists of those portions which the author believes may be considered autobiographical and which were contained in the first edition of this work. They have been revised by him to agree with his latest thinking, and some critical comments from the more recent book (translated into English) have been incorporated into this appendix. Notes numbered in arabic notation at the foot of the page are mainly Biblical citations as found in the original text of the French edition. Those indicated by alphabetical symbols are references to the author's more recent work and are found at the end of the chapter (Translator's note).

By an oath did I swear on my soul
To commit no sin against thee
And to do no wrong before thine eyes;
And so I progressed in the Community of the men of my
    counsel.ᵃ   (*Hymns* XIV:17-18)[1]

With great emphasis the Teacher of Righteousness recalls having been held in captivity and having known the feel of irons.

Whereas thou, O my God, didst inflate my spirit at large,
They (my enemies) did but add to my tribulation, and en-
    closed my soul in gloom.ᵇ
For I did in truth eat *sighing as my bread*[2]
And *my drink* (was) *mingled with* endless *tears.*[3]
For *my eyes wasted away because of grief*[4]
And my soul was in distress for *the blackness of the day.*[5]
[Fear] and affliction hemmed me in
And shame spread over my face.
My bread turned into dissension for me,ᶜ
My drink into reason for quarrels.

The[y[6] at]e into my very bones

---

[1] These hymns, which have so obviously been inspired by the Old Testament Scriptures in their thought and literary expression, are here set into English following the style (so far as possible) of the *Revised Standard Version.* Direct quotations have been set in italics and identified. The form of the rest of the text has been kept as compatible as possible *(Translator's note).*

[2] Reference to *Job* 3:24.   [3] *Ps.* 102:9.   [4] *Ps.* 6:7, or 31:9.
[5] *Job* 3:5.

[6] His food and drink, which, far from strengthening him, contributed only to his disablement.

To shake my spirit and crush my strength,
According to the secret ways of wickedness
Which, by their evil, transform the works of God.
For [I wa]s bound with unbreakable cords and with fetters
   not (to be) shattered—
A mi[ghty] bulwark [   ]
Barred with iron and with door[s of bronze].[7]

(*Hymns* V:32-37)

My soul is cast down within me[8] unto destruction,
For strength has deserted my body.
My heart *is poured out like water.*[9]
My flesh *melts like wax.*[10]
(And) the strength of my loins is become agitation.
My arm has been broken from its socket.[11]
[And (there is) no mean]s of moving the hand.
My fo[ot has been] caught in the net.[12]
My knees are become as water,[13]
And (there is) no (means) of extending the leg
Nor (of taking) a step to relieve the foot.
The [......]s of my arms *have been bound in chains*[14] that
   unbalance me.
A mighty (and) inexhaustible tongue hast thou put into my
   mouth,
(But I have) no (way) of ra[is]ing the voice and *the tongue*
   according to thy precepts,[15]
Of restoring breath to the spirit that falters
Or *of sustaining with a word him that is weary*[16] (for I am)
   a mute.

(*Hymns* VIII:32-37)

Next, the Teacher of Righteousness complains of having

[7] *Isaiah* 45:2.
[8] *Pss.* 42:6 and 43:5.   [9] *Ps.* 22:14.
[10] *Micah* 1:4 (or *Pss.* 22:14; 68:2; 97:5).   [11] *Job* 31:22.
[12] *Ps.* 9:15.   [13] *Ezekiel* 7:17.   [14] *Nahum* 3:10.
[15] *Isaiah* 50:4 (see p. 148, n. 137).   [16] *Ps.* 31:12.

135

been exiled, and he seems to make allusion to the banks of
the Nile:

> For he drove me from my country
> Like as a bird from its nest.
> All my companions and my friends
> Were driven far from me;
> They thought of me as of *one who is dead.*[17]
>
> (*Hymns* IV:8-9)

> I give thee thanks, O my Lord
> For that thou didst not abandon me
> During my exile among *a foreign people.*[d]
>
> (*Hymns* V:5)

[......] in the midst of lions[18] set apart *for the sons of guilt,*[e]
Lions that break all the bones[19] of the mighty
And *drink the blood of* the brave.[20]
Thou didst set me in (my) exile among many fishermen
Spreading their nets on the face of *the waters,*[21]
And (among) hunters after the children of savagery.[f]

(*Hymns* V:6-8)

The thoughts of the Teacher of Righteousness turn often
to his enemies, and he remembers with especial bitterness
the treachery of certain disciples:

And I was as a target [......],
Arguments and quarrels for my constant companions,[g]
Jealousy and anger as associates in my fellowship,
Gossip and criticism as those assembled about me.
[All *those who did*] *eat of my bread lifted their heel against
me.*[22]
They slandered me with a perverse tongue—
Even the associates of my fellowship.

[17] *Ps.* 31:12. [18] *Ps.* 57:4. [19] *Isaiah* 38:13. [20] *Numbers* 23:24.
[21] *Isaiah* 19:8.
[22] *Ps.* 41:9.

136

The men of my congregation made mutiny and criticized their
  surroundings.
As opposed to the secrecy which thou hast hidden in me,
They went hawking about to all the children of affliction.[h]

(*Hymns* V:22-25)

And they, the associates of my ministry,
They were seduced by the interpre[ters of falsehood]
And they have [......] *in the work of righteousness.*[23]
Thou, O God, hast ordained for (their) welfare (that they
  should go out) from their own ways
[To walk] in *the way of (thy) holiness,*[1]
Where *the uncircumcized, the unclean and the robber shall
  not pass over.*[24]
But they strayed from *the way of thy heart*[25]
And were *taken captive by their (own) lust.*[26]
After the manner of a counselor[27] Belial acts in their heart,
And following the devices of godlessness they wallow in their
  iniquity.   (*Hymns* VI:19-22)

On these deserters, as on his enemies, the Teacher of
Righteousness lays blame, above all else, for having perverted the people by their offenses:

The deceits of Belial [......] their devices
And they have pushed back down into the Pit the life of the
  man
In whose mouth thou hast placed thy doctrine,
(In whose) heart thou hast put wisdom,
To open the well-spring of knowledge to all who have under-
  standing.
But they have bartered these away for *uncircumcized lips*
And the *foreign speech*[j] of a people *without understanding,*

[23] *Isaiah* 32:17.
[24] *Isaiah* 52:1, then 35:8.   [25] *Isaiah* 57:17, and *Ecclesiastes* 11:9.
[26] *Proverbs* 11:6.   [27] *Nahum* 1:11.

In order *to lead them to ruin.*[28] (*Hymns* II:16-19)

My foot is sunk in the mire[29]
My eyes have turned aside *from looking upon evil*
And my *ears from hearing* (talk) *of bloodshed.*[30]
My heart was dismayed by the *schemes of the wicked,*[31]
For Belial partakes in the manifestation of their nature of evil.
All the foundations of my being were cracked
And my bones were out of joint[32];
My inward parts heaved like a boat in a stifling turbulence,
My heart beat wildly as if to self destruction,[33]
And *a wind of confusion*[34] swallowed me up
Because of the malice of their iniquity. (*Hymns* VII:2-5)

With more or less disillusionment the Teacher of
Righteousness reflects that he has served as a symbol of
contradiction—he has inspired some souls, but has aroused
only hatred in others:

I was *a snare to* wrongdoers[k]
And a source of healing[l] to *those who turn from transgression.*[35]
(I was) *prudence for the simple,*[36]
A *mind stayed (on thee)*[37] for them *of fearful heart.*[38]
Thou hast made of me *a byword and a laughing-stock*[39] for
    traitors,
A counsel of truth and wisdom for *those who walk uprightly.*[40]
I was in arms against the iniquity of the wicked,
A name of depravity on the lips of madmen,

---

[28] This verse combines elements borrowed from *Exodus* 6:12,
Isaiah 33:19, and from *Hoseah* 4:14.   [29] *Jeremiah* 38:22.
    [30] *Isaiah* 33:15, influenced by 32:3.
    [31] *Ezekiel* 38:10, or *Proverbs* 15:26.   [32] *Ps.* 22:14.
    [33] *Jeremiah* 4:19.
    [34] *Isaiah* 19:14. (R.S.V. reads: spirit of confusion.)
    [35] *Isaiah* 59:20.   [36] *Proverbs* 1:4, or 8:5.   [37] *Isaiah* 26:3.
    [38] *Isaiah* 35:4.   [39] *Ps.* 44:14.   [40] *Ps.* 37:14.

Wastrels, *gnashing their teeth.*[41]
As for me, *I became the song*[42] of offenders;
Against me snarled the pack of the wicked,
And they roared like the thundering of the seas[43]
When their waves roll, *tossing up mire and dirt.*[44]
Thou hast made me a beacon[m] for the elect of righteousness[n]
And an interpreter of wisdom in wonderful secrets,
To test thy disciples in the truth
And to try those *who love discipline.*[45]
I was *a man of contention*[46] for the interpreters of the wrong
  way,
But a [man of pea]ce to the seers of truth.[47]
I was a *spirit of jealousy*[48] against the seekers after com-
  [promise[o]
And all] the men of cowardice raged against me
Like the voice of the roaring of mighty waters.

(*Hymns* II:8-16)

The Teacher of Righteousness was so deeply hurt by his
tribulations, and especially by certain insults, that he
describes them again in moving terms:

This became (such) an *inconsolable pain*[49]
And *malignant disease*[50]
In the viscera of thy servant
As to cause [the spirit] *to fail*
And to wear away *strength,*[51]
So as no longer to hold fast (thy) position.
They *have overtaken me*[52] in defiles with no way of escape
And without a way of breaking (their) hold.
They have lampooned my opposition on the lyre
(And) on a chorus of instruments (expressed) their censure.

[41] *Ps.* 37:12.   [42] *Job* 30:9, or 3:14.   [43] *Isaiah* 17:12.
[44] *Isaiah* 57:20.   [45] *Proverbs* 12:1.   [46] *Jeremiah* 15:10.
[47] *Isaiah* 30:10.   [48] *Numbers* 5:14 and 30.
[49] *Isaiah* 17:11.   [50] *Leviticus* 13:51.   [51] *Lamentations* 1:14.
[52] *Lamentations* 1:3.

With *distress and anguish*[53]
Consternation (seized me)[54]
And convulsions *like the pangs of a woman in travail.*[55]
My heart moaned over this matter[56]
I clothed myself *with blackness*[57]
And *my tongue cleaved to the roof of my mouth.*[58]
[..... ....] their heart,
Their nature became apparent to me in bitterness,
The light of my countenance[59] became shadowed in obscurity
And *my radiant appearance was changed*[60] into despondency.

(*Hymns* V:28-32)

I was as a sailor on a ship amidst the *raging* of *the seas*[61];
Their *waves and all* their *billows* roared *over me.*[62]
There was a *wind of confusion,*[63] with no time for *catching*
(my) *breath*[64]
Nor any *path to show a way on the face of the waters.*[65]
The depth shook with my groaning
And [my] so[u]l [......] even *to the gates of death.*[66]
But I was as one who enters *into a fortified city*
And takes refuge on *a high wall*[67] until (his) deliverance.

(*Hymns* VI:22-25)

The waves of death[68] and of Sheol (rolled) over *the bed* of
my *slumbers.*[69]
In lamentation my soul lifts up *the voice of my complaint.*[70]
My eyes (are like) the [f]ire in a furnace
And my *tears like torrents* of water.[71]
My eyes are (too) *spent*[72] for repose;

[53] *Zephaniah* 1:15.
[54] *Ps.* 119:53 (R.S.V. reads: hot indignation seized me.)
[55] *Isaiah* 21:3.   [56] *Jeremiah* 48:36.   [57] *Isaiah* 50:3.
[58] *Ps.* 137:6.   [59] *Ps.* 90:8.   [60] *Daniel* 10:8.
[61] *Jonah* 1:15.   [62] *Ps.* 42:7.
[63] *Isaiah* 19:14 (R.S.V. reads: spirit of confusion.)
[64] *Lamentations* 1:11.   (R.S.V. reads: to revive their strength.)
[65] *Isaiah* 43:16, combined with *Genesis* 1:2.   [66] *Ps.* 107:18.
[67] *Isaiah* 30:13.   [68] *2 Samuel* 22:5.   [69] *Ps.* 132:3-4.
[70] *Ps.* 102:5 (R.S.V. reads: my loud groaning.)
[71] *Lamentations* 2:18.   [72] *Lamentations* 2:11.

[Sleep] stays far away from me
And my life (is) in loneliness. (*Hymns* IX:4-6)

But the Teacher of Righteousness was always marvelously sustained and delivered by God, to whom he offers
all his gratitude:

I give thee thanks, O my Lord,
For thine eye hath [......] all my soul
And thou hast delivered me from the jealousy of the inter-
   preters of falsehood,
And from the congregation of the seekers after compromise.
Thou hast *delivered the life of the needy*,[73]
Whose blood they were preparing to waste,
Pouring it out because of thy service.
Nevertheless, they [......] that my steps (come) from thee,
And they *made a mockery of* me, and a *reproach*
In the mouth of all seekers after dissipation.
Thou, O my God, hast assisted the soul *of the afflicted and the
   destitute*[74]
(To escape) *the hand of one stronger than himself*,[75]
And hast redeemed my soul from the hands of the mighty.
Amidst their jeers thou hast not let me be so much afraid
As to abandon thy service from dread of *the harassing of the
   wicked*,[76]
Nor to barter away in foolishness the steadfast spirit which
   thou hast given me. (*Hymns* II:31-36)

In the eyes of the Teacher of Righteousness the providential reason for the trials that beset him was to furnish
God the occasion for glorifying Himself by the deliverance of the righteous and the punishment of the wicked:

---

[73] *Jeremiah* 20:13. [74] *Ps.* 82:3.
[75] *Jeremiah* 31:11 (R.S.V. reads: from hands too strong for
him.)
[76] *Proverbs* 10:3 (R.S.V. reads: the craving of the wicked.)

I give thee thanks, O my Lord,
For that thou hast placed my soul in the treasure-chest[p] of life,
And hast protected me against the snares of the Pit.
For riotous men *sought in my life to destroy it*:[77]
But I trusted in thy covenant.
For they, the council of nothingness and the congregation of
Belial,
They know not that because of thee I stand upright,
And that *in thy love thou savest my life*.[78]
For because of thee (do I continue on) my course.
Only according to thy will have they led their assault against
my life,
That thou mightest be glorified in the judgment of the ungodly,
And mightest be magnified in me before the children of men;
For by thy favor do I stand upright.   (*Hymns* II:20-25)

For me, when my heart *melted and became as water*,[79]
My soul *held fast thy covenant*.[80]
As for them, *in the net which they hide shall their own foot
be caught*.[81]
And the traps which they have concealed against my life shall
fall upon them.
My foot stands on level ground;
(*In*) their *congregations I shall bless* thy name.[82]

                                        (*Hymns* II:28-30)

Thou hast closed the mouth of the lions' whelps,
Whose *teeth* are like *swords*
And whose *fangs* like pointed *spears*.[83]
All their devices (were) *the poison of serpents*[84];
They *lay in wait like robbers*[85]
But did not *open their mouths at me*.[86]

[77] A common enough Biblical phrase.
[78] *Ps.* 6:4, and 31:16.   [79] *Joshua* 7:5.   [80] *Isaiah* 56:4.
[81] *Ps.* 9:15.   [82] *Ps.* 26:12.   [83] *Ps.* 57:4.
[84] *Deuteronomy* 32:33.   [85] *Proverbs* 23:28.   [86] *Ps.* 22:13.

For thou, O my God, hast given me *refuge in the sight of the sons of men*[87];
And thou hast hidden thy law [within me
Unt]il the time of the *revelation* of thy *salvation*[q] *for me.*[88]
For in *the distress of my soul*[89] thou didst not abandon me;
Thou *didst hear my cry*[90] in the bitterness of my soul
And didst listen to the voice of my affliction in my complaint.
Thou *hast delivered the life of the needy*[91] from *the lions' den,*[92]
Whose tongues were whetted like swords.[93]
Thou, O my god, didst muzzle their teeth
Lest they rend[94] the soul of *the afflicted and the destitute.*[95]
Thou didst make their tongue *return as a sword into its scabbard,*
Without thy having [. . . . . .] *the soul of thy servant.*
In order to magnify thyself in me *in the sight of the sons of men,*[96]
Thou hast acted wondrously toward the needy.
Thou hast put him into the fur[nace like go]ld[97] tried by fire,[r]
Like silver molten in a crucible (heated) with bellows,[98]
purified seven times.[99]
The (most) ungodly among the mighty hurled themselves upon me with their tortures,
And all day long they crushed my spirit.
But thou, O my God, *madest the storm be still*[100]
And didst deliver the *soul of the needy* like [. . . . . .]
(As) prey snatched from *the jaws of lions.*   (*Hymns* V:9-19)

As for me, whether *in calamity or disaster,*[101]
Whether in sickness or in disease,
In torments or in broken bones,
My soul *meditates*[s] *on thy wondrous works.*[102]

---

[87] *Ps.* 31:19.   [88] Inspired, perhaps, by *Isaiah* 56:1.
[89] *Genesis* 42:21.   [90] *Ps.* 40:1.   [91] *Jeremiah* 20:3.
[92] *Nahum* 2:11.   [93] *Ps.* 64:3.   [94] *Ps.* 7:2.   [95] *Ps.* 82:3.
[96] *Ps.* 31:19.   [97] *Proverbs* 27:21.
[98] Reference to *Ezekiel* 22:20.   [99] *Ps.* 12:6.   [100] *Ps.* 107:29.
[101] *Zephaniah* 1:15.   [102] *Ps.* 119:27.

Thou hast not withdrawn thy favor from me, moment by
   moment;
My soul is *cheered by thy consolations,*[103] and the greatness of
   thy compassion.[104]
I gave *answer* to *him* who would have swallowed me up
And defiance to him who threw himself upon me.
I declared his case unrighteous,
And I declare thy sentence just;
For I have recognized thy truth;
I have assented to my sentence,
And I have accepted my ordeal;
For I have put my hope in thy favors.
Thou hast placed a supplication in the mouth of thy servant;
Thou hast not repudiated my hope;
Thou hast not kept my peace far from me[105]*;*
Thou hast not rejected my expectation,
And under the scourge thou hast sustained my spirit.
For (it is) thou (who) hast established my spirit,
Thou hast known my intention,
And hast consoled me in my tribulation.
I have delighted in thy pardons,
As if they consoled me for the original fault.
I have known that there is hope in thy kindnesses
And confidence in the abundance of thy strength.

                                          (*Hymns* IX:6-14)

In short, the Teacher of Righteousness emerged victorious from these trials, and they contributed to the
radiance of his spirit:

Thou hast exalted my horn[106] over all my detractors;
They were [. . . . . .], the men warring against me,[107]
And those (*contending*) with *me*[108] *like chaff before the
   wind.*[109]

   [103] *Ps.* 94:19.
   [104] *Isaiah* 63:15.   [105] *Lamentations* 3:17.   [106] *Ps.* 92:10.
   [107] *Isaiah* 41:11–12.   [108] *Isaiah* 50:8.
   [109] *Isaiah* 17:13, or *Ps.* 35:5.

My dominion [. . . . . .] against them who deride me,
Against my [. . . . . .] thou hast succoured my soul,
Thou hast exalted my horns ever higher and higher[110]
And I appeared in *the sevenfold light.*[111]
Thou hast strengthened my [. . . . . .] by thy glory,
For thou art for me *an everlasting light*[112]
And hast strengthened my feet in thy paths.

(*Hymns* VII:22-25)

In the secret of thy wisdom hast thou rebuked me
And hast hidden the truth [. . . . . .] its time.
Thy rebuke has become for me a joy and a delight,
My adversity a cure [. . . . . .] forever,
The scorn of my enemies for me a crown of glory,
And my weakness an everlasting strength.
For in [. . . . . .] and in thy glory has my light appeared
For out of the darkness thou hast made a light to shine,
[. . . . . . the e]nd of my scourging,
And in place of my stumbling, a marvelous strength.

(*Hymns* IX:23-27)

The enemies of the Teacher of Righteousness would be punished, while, on the other hand, his disciples would share in his triumph and the extermination of the ungodly:

For all my assailants *shalt thou confute in judgment,*[113]
So as to *distinguish,* through me *between the righteous and the wicked.*[114]
For thou didst *understand all* (the) *nature of* (their) *action*[115]
And perceive all *the answers of their tongue.*[116]

---

110 *Ps.* 92:10.
111 Allusion to *Isaiah* 30:26.   112 *Isaiah* 60:19–20.
113 *Isaiah* 54:17.   114 *Malachi* 3:18.
115 *Deuteronomy* 31:21. (R.S.V. reads: the purposes which they are already forming.)
116 *Proverbs* 16:1.

Thou didst establish my heart [in] thy [pre]cepts and in thy
  truth,
To guide my feet in *the way of righteousness*,[117]
To walk before thee in the land of [the li]ving
In paths of glory and peace without bou[nd],
(Which will) n[ot] (have) to end, for all eternity.

(Hymns VII 12-15)

For me, because I put my trust in thee,
I shall arise and stand upright[118] before them that deride me,
My hand above all my scorners,
For they held me in no esteem until thou didst triumph in me.
Thou hast appeared to me in thy strength at daybreak,
And hast not besmeared my face with shame.
All those who trust[ed] in me have joined together in thy
  covenant.
They listened to me, those who walked in the way of thy
  heart,
And they volunteered on thy side in the company of the saints.
Thou hast *made their justice go forth* in brilliance,[119]
And their truth in equity.
Thou wilt not let them be led astray by the hand of reprobates,
As had been their intention towards them;
Thou hast *laid the fear of* them *upon*[120] thy people
And destruction for *all the peoples of other lands*,[121]
To execute judgment on all *the transgressors*[t] *of thy com-
  mand.*[122]

(Hymns IV:22-27)

I know that *there is hope*[123]
For those who turn from transgression[124] and abandon sin,
When [they ....]
And when *they walk in the way of thy heart*[125] *without in-
  iquity.*[126]

---

[117] *Proverbs* 12:28.
[118] *Ps.* 20:8.
[119] The author refers to *Habakkuk* 1:4, but turns the negative
into an affirmative of triumph.
[120] *Deuteronomy* 11:25. [121] *2 Chronicles* 32:13.
[122] *Numbers* 14:41. [123]*Ezra* 10:2. [124] *Isaiah* 59:20.
[125] *Ecclesiastes* 11:9. [126] *Deuteronomy* 32:4.

I was consoled by the *tumult of the people,*
The uproar of kingdoms at the time of their *gathering to-*
gether.[127]
[For] I [k]new that in *a little while*[128] thou wouldst deliver
the survivors of thy people and the *remnant of thy herit-*
age,[129]
And that thou hadst refined them that they might be pure of
(all) offense.   (*Hymn* VI:6–8)

For the Teacher of Righteousness was conscious of
fulfilling a providential mission and accomplishing a
wonderful work:

Through me thou hast illuminated the countenance of many
And hast increased them *beyond number.*[130]
For thou hast instructed me in thy marvelous secrets
And in thy marvelous counsel thou hast fortified my stand;
It has appeared marvelous in the sight of many, in view of
thy glory,
And *to make known to all who live*[u] *Thy mighty deeds.*[131]
                                                 (*Hymn* IV:27-29)

I give thee thanks, O my Lord!
For thou hast sustained me with thy strength
And hast poured out upon me *thy spirit of holiness*[132]*;*
I shall not be moved.[133]
Thou hast armed me against the ways of the ungodly . . .
    thou hast made of me *a strong tower*[134]
[Like] *a high wall*[135]*;*
And in spite of all their devices they have not obstructed thy
covenant.

---

[127] *Isaiah* 13:4.   [128] *Isaiah* 63:18.
[129] *2 Kings* 21:14, or *Micah* 7:18.
[130] Reference to *Ps.* 40:12.   [131] *Ps.* 145:12.
[132] *Isaiah* 63:10, 11; or *Ps.* 51:11 (R.S.V. reads: thy holy Spirit.)
[133] *Ps.* 10:6, or 16:8.   [134] *Ps.* 61:3, or *Proverbs* 18:10.
[135] *Isaiah* 30:13, or *Proverbs* 18:11.

Thou hast made fast on the rock my house
And the eternal foundations of my fellowship;
All my walls form a rampart, proven (and) unshakable.
Thou, O my God, hast given it[136] (to be) for the weary a
  council of holiness,
And thou hast [. . . . . .] according to thy covenant, and my
  tongue according to thy precepts.[137]   (*Hymns* VII:6-10)

. . . to make a shoot grow up
To preserve [. . . . . .] in strength.
[In] thy righteousness thou hast appointed me for thy cove-
nant
That I may hold fast in the truth
And that I [. . . . . .].
Thou hast made me a father to the children of grace
And like a guardian to *men of good omen*.[138]
They have opened their mouth like the nursling,
And like *the sucking child*[139] in *the bosom of its nurses*.[140]
                                   (*Hymns* VII:19-22)

To describe the benefits of his influence, the Teacher of
Righteousness turns to the Biblical image of an oasis
surrounding a spring:

I [give thee thanks, O] my Lord!
For thou hast made me a wellspring of *streams on the dry
land*,[141]
A spring of water on *the thirsty ground*.[142]
A well watered garden[143] [. . . . .] wreath,
A planting of *pines*, of *planes*,
And also of *cypress*, brought together for thy *glory*[144];

---

[136] The house, or the fellowship?
[137] *Isaiah* 50:4 (R.S.V. reads: the tongue of those who are
taught.)
[138] *Zechariah* 3:8.   [139] Following *Isaiah* 11:8.
[140] Following *Numbers* 11:12.   [141] *Isaiah* 44:3, 41:18.
[142] *Isaiah* 35:7.
[143] Following *Genesis* 13:10.   [144] *Isaiah* 60:13.

Trees of life[v] close to the secret spring
(Are) hidden amongst all *the trees (that drink) water*,[145]
And they will have to make a shoot grow up for an eternal
    planting,
To root it before making it grow.
They will *send out their roots by the stream*[146]
So that the stem shall absorb *the* living *waters*
And share in the eternal fountain.
On the shoot[147] (grown) beside this (fountain) shall all [the
    beasts of] the forest[148] feed;
The garden about its stem (shall be) for *all who pass along the
    way*,[149]
And its branches for *every winged bird*.[150]
Near (this fountain) shall grow tall all *the trees (that drink)
    water*.[151]   (*Hymns* VIII:4-9)

       Thou, O my God, hast placed in my mouth
       As it were a freshet of *the autumn rain*[152]
       And a *spring of* living *waters*.[153]
                     (*Hymns* VIII:16-17)

However, the Teacher of Righteousness never lets himself become obsessed with pride, and he retains a vivid
understanding of human wretchedness.

I—(a creature) modelled of clay (and) kneaded with water,
The coming together of degradation and the flow of pollution,
The sink of iniquity and the framework of sin,
The spirit of errancy and [. . . ?]
Perverted, without understanding, and terrified by the judg-
    ments of righteousness[154]

---

[145] *Ezekiel* 31:14.   [146] *Jeremiah* 17:8.
[147] The following passage is a development of *Ezekiel* 31:16.
[148] *Isaiah* 56:9.
[149] *Pss.* 80:12; 89:41; *Lamentations* 1:12; 2:15.
[150] *Genesis* 1:21.   [151] *Ezekiel* 31:14.   [152] *Jeremiah* 5:24.
[153] *Isaiah* 35:7.
[154] This phrase occurs seven times in the Bible.

What shall I say that is not known?
And (what) shall I proclaim that has not been told?
(*Hymns* I:21-23)

I, (who am but) dust and ashes[155]—
What (can) I plan, unless thou hast willed it,
And what (can) I decide, apart from thy good pleasure?
(With) what (can) I arm myself, unless thou sustainest me,
And how (can) I have wisdom, unless thou hast formed (it in)
    me?
What can I preach, unless thou hast opened my mouth,
And how (can) I answer, unless thou givest me wisdom?
(*Hymns* X:5-7)

The Teacher of Righteousness does not flinch even from recognizing himself as a sinner, albeit one who has been purified according to the divine mercy:

I (am a very member) of ungodly humanity,
Of the carnal fellowship of unrighteousness;
My iniquities, my faults, my sin,
Together with the *perversity of my mind*,[156]
(Relate me) to the species of vermin, to (the creatures that)
    crawl in darkness.   (*Rule of the Community* XI:9-10)

For my part, *trembling* and terror have *seized*[157] me,
All my bones are creaking,
My heart is melted like wax before the fire,[158]
My knees are become[159] *like waters poured down a steep*
    place.[160]
For I remember my offenses,
As well as the faithlessness of my forefathers,
When the ungodly rose up against thy covenant,
And the guilty against thy word.
And I said:

[155] *Genesis* 18:27, or *Job* 30:19.   [156] *Proverbs* 12:8.
[157] *Isaiah* 33:14, or *Ps.* 48:6.
[158] *Ps.* 22:14, combined with *Micah* 1:4.   [159] *Ezekiel* 7:17.
[160] *Micah* 1:4.

Because of my sins I am forsaken, outside thy covenant.
But, when I remembered *the strength of thy hand*,[161]
And also the number of thy kindnesses,
I *arose and stood upright*,[162]
And my spirit was established in (its) stand in the face of the
    ordeal.
For I found rest in thy favors
And in the number of thy kindnesses.
For thou *forgivest iniquity*.[163]
So that the human (being) may be purified of sin by thy
    righteousness.   (*Hymns* IV:33-37)

Not according to my offenses hast thou judged me,
Nor hast thou abandoned me to the inclinations of my nature;
Thou hast preserved *my life from the Pit*.[164]   (*Hymns* V:5-6)

Furthermore, the Teacher of Righteousness sees in God
the source of all the favors with which he has been
showered:

As for me, my righteousness (comes from) God;
In his hand, the perfection of my way, with the uprightness
    of my heart;
And by his righteousness he wipes away my sins.
For from the wellspring of his wisdom has poured forth my
    light,
My eye has contemplated his marvels
And the light of my heart (pierces even) unto the secret of the
    future.
The eternal Being (is) the support of my right hand,
On a solid rock (lies) the way of my footsteps;
They shall not be moved for any (cause).
For God's truth is the rock of my footsteps;
His might, the support of my right hand,
And from the wellspring of his righteousness (comes) my
    justification.

[161] *Isaiah* 10:13.   [162] *Ps.* 20:8.
[163] *Ps.* 78:38.   [164] *Jonah* 2:6.

The light in my heart (comes) from his marvelous secrets,
My eye has beheld the eternal Being:
Skill which is concealed from man to know,
Knowledge of proficiency beyond the (reach of) the children
 of men!
Source of Righteousness and Reservoir of Might,
With the Fountain of Glory beyond the (reach of) carnal
 humanity!
To those whom God has chosen,
He has given an eternal possession,
He has granted (them) the portion of the saints.
With the sons of Heaven he has joined their fellowship,
For the counsel of the Community, the foundation of the holy
 building,
The eternal planting enduring through all ages to come . . .
For his way (belongs) not to man (himself),
(And *it is*) not (*in*) *man to direct his steps.*[165]
For to God (belongs) the verdict,
And from his hand (comes) perfection of conduct.
By his wisdom all things have (their) existence.
He established everything there is according to his plan,
And without him was not anything made.
And I, if I falter,
The mercies of God will be my salvation forever;
If I stumble in the iniquity of the flesh,
My justification will be in the righteousness of God, established
 forever;
If he opens my tribulation,
He will *deliver my soul from the Pit,*[166]
And he will guide my *footsteps in the way.*[167]
He has pursued me with loving kindnesses,
And from his mercies shall come my justification.
He has judged me in the righteousness of his truth,
And in the multitude of his goodness he will pardon all my
 iniquities.

[165] *Jeremiah* 10:23.
[166] *Ps.* 116:8 combined with *Isaiah* 38:17.   [167] *Ps.* 85:13.

In his righteousness he will purify me from mortal stain
And from (the) sin of the children of men,
So as to glorify God for his righteousness
And the Most High for his magnificence.

(Rule of the Community XI:2–15)

Likewise, the Teacher of Righteousness wishes to consecrate himself wholly to the praise and glory of the divine Majesty:

I would sing with skill;
All my music shall be for the glory of God,
My lyre (and) my harp for the rule of his holiness;
I shall lift up the flute of my lips to the measure of his decree.
With the coming of day and night
I would enter into the covenant of God;
With the going of evening and morning
I shall recite his commandments;
In their existence I establish my uttermost bounds
(From which there shall be) no receding;
I shall believe his judgment proper for my transgressions
And my sins (shall be measured) in my own eyes according
   to his commandment(s) graven (on stone).
To God, I say: O my Righteousness!
And to the Most High: O thou Source of all my Good!
Wellspring of Wisdom, Fountain of Holiness,
Height of Glory, Almighty of Eternal Splendor;
I would choose that which he teaches me;
I would love that which he awards.
Whenever I put forth hand or foot
I shall bless his name.
Whenever I go out or come in,
When I sit down or stand up,
Or when I lay me down on my bed,
I shall exult in him and shall bless him,
(With) the offering issuing from my lips,
Because of the table spread before men.
Before I raise my hands

To nourish myself with the delights of the produce of earth,
In the moment of fright and terror,
In the place of agony and desolation,
I shall bless him in his increasing marvels
And shall glorify his might.
By his mercies I shall be supported all the day long,
And I shall know that the judgment of all things living is in
 his hand
And that all his works (are) truth.
At the beginning of agony I shall laud him
And at deliverance I shall exult likewise.

(*Rule of the Community* X:9-17)

The fervor of his piety finally leads the Teacher of
Righteousness, inspired by the Old Testament, to discover
in God the most beautiful of all titles—that of "Father":

For thou, more than my father, hast understood me;
More than the bosom [......,]
More than my mother hast thou cared for me,
More than the breasts of her that conceived me (are) thy
 loving kindnesses towards me,
And in the lap of her who bare me [......]
From my youth upward thou hast appeared to me in the wis-
 dom of thy judgment,
In steadfast truth thou hast sustained me,
In thy spirit of holiness thou delightest me.
Until the day of [......,]
The rebuke of thy righteousness with my [......,]
The observance of thy peace for the safe-guarding of my soul.
With my footsteps the multitude of thy pardons,
The number of thy loving-kindnesses in thy judgment of me,
And until my old age it is thou who wilt encompass me.
For my father did not understand me
And *my mother has abandoned me*[168] to thee.
For thou art a father[169] to all the children of truth
And thou hast rejoiced over[170] them as a mother over her babe;

[168] *Ps.* 27:10.   [169] *Isaiah* 63:16.   [170] *Zephaniah* 3:17.

And as one who carries the sucking child[171] in his bosom,
So dost thou encompass thy creation.ʷ

(*Hymns* IX, 29-36)

EXPLANATORY NOTES ON THE HYMNS

ᵃ "I progressed," literally, "I made myself progress" or "I made progress." As in the French word "conseil," the Hebrew SWD may mean either the deliberation or the group which deliberates. Thus we may understand "the men who share my opinions, my ideal," or "the men who form with me a single group"; but in the present case these two translations mean almost the same thing. The passage indicates both that the Teacher of Righteousness is the leader of the Community and that he arrived at this post progressively. Therefore he was not the founder (as is also shown by the *Damascus Document* I, 9–11). (*Les Textes de Qumran*, p. 156, n. 17)

ᵇ The author describes his detention in a dungeon . . . unless all this development is to be taken in a metaphorical sense (*Ibid.*, p. 219, n. 31).

ᶜ Either the author had to fight to obtain his food and drink, or these quarrels had become for him as lasting as his need of eating and drinking (*Ibid.*, p. 219, n. 36).

ᵈ *Ex.* 21:8. This exile would seem to be different from that seeking of refuge to which allusion was made in IV, 8–9 above. Then seemingly the author had need only to hide for a time, but this time he had to take flight even to a foreign country to escape his persecutors (*Ibid.*, p. 213, n. 2).

ᵉ The "sons of guilt" are the guilty condemned to the wild beasts. The author sees himself in the situation of Daniel in the lions' den (*Dan.* 6:17–25; 14:30–41; *Ibid.*, p. 213, n. 6).

ᶠ These references and metaphors suggest that the author had possibly taken refuge on the banks of the Nile. The children of savagery are wild beasts. The author deliberately chose a formula which echoed the "sons of guilt" in the preceding passage (*Ibid.*, p. 214, n. 9).

[171] Following *Numbers* 11:12.

155

ᵍ All this passage is evidential proof that the author of the *Hymns* is the principal leader of the Community, and thus obviously the Teacher of Righteousness (*Ibid.*, p. 217, n. 6).

ʰ This whole passage clearly alludes to a mutiny provoked within the Community (*Ibid.*, p. 217, n. 12).

ⁱ The author superposes *Is.* 48:17, 'I am the Lord your God, who teaches you to profit, who leads you in the way you should go"; *Deut.* 13:6 (R.S.V. 13:5), "the way in which the Lord your God commanded you to walk"; and *Is.* 35:8, "it shall be called the Holy Way." Furthermore, he reproduces *Is.* 48:17 according to a curious variant of the second Isaiah scroll of Cave I, MDRKYK, "out of Thy ways" rather than MDRYKK, "he who leads you" (inversion of two letters). The meaning is clear: it is in their own interest that God has prescribed to the members of the Community that they should leave their wicked ways and set forth in the way of holiness (*Ibid.*, p. 223, n. 74).

ʲ This foreign speech was probably Aramaic, and then the author was making allusion to the early efforts to translate or to comment on the inspired books in the popular language. Further, this reproach seems to fall on the Pharisees, authors of *Midrashim* and *Targums*. This rigidity relaxed later even at Qumran, since the *Genesis Apocryphon* has been found there, written in Aramaic (*Ibid.*, p. 187, n. 117).

ᵏ *Is.* 8:14, "He (Yahweh) will be a snare . . . to the inhabitants of Jerusalem." The whole of this verse seems to have inspired both *Lk.* 2:34–35 and the rest of our poem. Like *Jeremiah* (1:10) and later like Jesus the author has become a sign of contradiction which obliges every heart to expose its inward disposition. In a series of antitheses the author here paints for us his role and his mission (*Ibid.*, p. 185, n. 90).

ˡ The author places "healing" at the head of all his good deeds, just as, in the *Rule of the Community*, IV, 6, it is the first of the rewards accorded the righteous. This would be particularly understandable if "Essene" actually means "healer" as G. Vermes thinks ("The Etymology of Essenes," *Revue de Qumran*, t. II, no. 3, p. 427-443) (*Les Textes de Qumran*, p. 185, n. 91).

[m] This image of the standard raised as a rallying signal is doubtless borrowed from *Isaiah*, who applied it to the "rod of Jesse" (the Davidic Messiah) in 11:10. But, in *Isaiah*, this image is always associated with a universalist context (5:26; 11:10, 12; 13:2; 18:3; 49:22; 62:10) where it is a matter of calling together even the pagan nations; whereas here, the author envisions only the assembly of "lovers of discipline" (*Ibid.*, p. 186, n. 101).

[n] This is to say, the elect destined to do righteousness, to be of the righteous, just as in the *Rule of the Community*, XII, 1, the "elect of the people of holiness" are the elect destined to take part in the true Israel. This "election" is opposed to that of which St. Paul speaks (*Rom.* 9:11; 11:5, 7, 28) just as the "righteousness" of Qumran is opposed to "righteousness" according to St. Paul (*Ibid.*, p. 186, n. 102).

[o] A related turn of phrase is found in *Is.* 30:10 . . . The same title reappears in II, 32; in the 3rd *Isaiah Commentary*, line 10 (commenting on *Is.* 30:18); in the *Nahum Commentary* lines 2 and 7 (commenting on *Nahum* 2:12–13); and an equivalent in the *Damascus Document*, 1, 18, to stigmatize those who would not push their rigidity far enough—probably referring to the Pharisees. On the reverse side, the *Talmud*, which represents the thinking of the Pharisees, may perhaps be making allusion to the men of Qumran when it refers to "seekers of heavy burdens" (see C. Roth, *Revue de Qumran*, t. II, no. 2, p. 261-265) (*Ibid.*, p. 187, n. 110).

[p] *I Sam.* 25:29. Literally: "in the purse of life," that is to say, "Thou hast watched over my life as attentively as one watches over the money in his purse" (*Ibid.*, p. 188, n. 2).

[q] This can be understood either as "the revelation to me of thy salvation" or "the revelation of thy salvation for me" (*Ibid.*, p. 215, n. 20).

[r] The image of the "furnace" is common at Qumran for describing "fiery" trials, especially those inflicted on the righteous under the domination of Belial. . . . In this passage (the author) clearly sets forth his theology of suffering. God permits the trials of the righteous in order to manifest His power in their deliverance (*Ibid.*, p. 215, n. 30).

[s] This magnificent passage shows that, for the author, man's suffering served essentially to furnish God with the occasion for spectacular deliverance. Nowhere, it seems, does the author even appear to suspect that suffering could have a value of oblation or redemption, although these ideas had already been found in the Suffering Servant poems of Isaiah and were basic to Christianity (*Ibid.*, p. 243, n. 75).

[t] These transgressors, then, are not only the pagans, but also those Israelites disobedient to the teachings of the author. This is exactly the point of view of the *War Scroll* I, 2 (*Ibid.*, p. 209, n. 46).

[u] *Ps.* 145:12. The author replaces "the sons of men" by "all who live." The context seems to indicate that it is the author who is supposed to "act marvelously" and "to make known to all who live"; but these words could also be applied to God, translating "in acting marvelously" and "in making known . . ." (*Ibid.*, p. 209, n. 50).

[v] *Gen.* 2:9 or *Prov.* 3:18. It is astonishing that the author does not speak of the "tree of life" in the singular (as is done in *Genesis* and *Proverbs*); but the *Psalms of Solomon* also employs the plural, stating that the "trees of life (are) the saints (of the Lord)" (*Ibid.*, p. 237, n. 6).

[w] *Num.* 11:12. This poem equals, or perhaps surpasses, the most beautiful passages of the Old Testament on the fatherhood of God. Although this theme was rarely treated at Qumran (here only, so far as is known) the author professes so profound a tenderness that his filial confidence becomes as it were a prelude to the Our Father (*Matt.* 6:9) and to various passages of the New Testament (*Lk.* 15:11–32; *Ephes.* 3:15). Nevertheless, the author seems able to envisage the fatherhood of God only towards "His faithful children" whereas in the Gospel it is extended even to sinners, and in fact the plants and animals experience its blessings (*Matt.* 6:26–30; *Ibid.*, p. 247, n. 116).

Bibliography for the General Reader

Selected and annotated by KATHARINE GREENLEAF PEDLEY

Allegro, John Marco. *People of the Dead Sea Scrolls,* Doubleday, 1958.

This is a popular book, consisting of plates and only 51 pages of text. It is by far the best pictorial presentation of Qumran. The author has modified some of his earlier extreme views, but still states as fact the martyrdom of the Teacher of Righteousness and fails to mention that this is a hypothesis with which many scholars can not agree.

Bruce, Frederick F. *Second Thoughts on the Dead Sea Scrolls,* Eerdmans, 1956.

The author is Professor of Biblical history and literature at the University of Sheffield. His book has been called the best and most readable published in England. His position on controversial points is moderate and in line with the majority opinion.

Burrows, Millar. *Dead Sea Scrolls,* Viking, 1955.
More light on the Dead Sea Scrolls: New scrolls and new interpretations, Viking, 1958.

These two volumes together constitute *the* most complete and scholarly work on the subject. The author, Director of the American School of Oriental Research in Jerusalem at the time of the discovery, not only tells the story of the finding of the scrolls and fragments and the excavating of the buildings, but reviews most of the literature that has grown up around the Qumran texts, and gives his own translation of many of them. These books are for scholars rather than casual readers.

Cross, Frank Moore, Jr. *Ancient Library of Qumran and Modern Biblical Studies*, Doubleday, 1958.

The best single volume work of the subject by an American. Professor Cross of Harvard Divinity School is one of the scholars actually engaged in work on the scrolls in Jerusalem, and he speaks with first hand knowledge. This has recently been reissued in a paper-back edition.

Daniélou, Jean. *Dead Sea Scrolls and Primitive Christianity*, Helicon, 1959; Mentor Omega, 1962.

Father Daniélou has written a fascinating and provocative book on a highly controversial problem. Many Catholic reviewers have given only qualified approval to his thesis, although admiring the brilliance of his writing.

Fritsch, Charles T. *Qumrân Community: Its History and Scrolls*, Macmillan, 1956.

One of the best books on the subject. The author is Professor of Old Testament at Princeton.

Gaster, Theodor H., ed. & tr. *Dead Sea Scriptures*, Doubleday, 1956.

One of the first translations made available to the general public, and the first at a popular price. Unfortunately, later finds of fragments have made some of his readings obsolete, and he himself would undoubtedly make many changes today. Nevertheless, the literary quality of this translation does honor to Jewish scholarship.

Graystone, Geoffrey. *Dead Sea Scrolls and the Originality of Christ*, Sheed and Ward, 1956.

A good book on a difficult topic. *Commonweal* complains that Father Graystone has erred in the direction of conservatism. Thus his book is a striking contrast to that of Father Daniélou.

Harrison, R. K. *The Dead Sea Scrolls; an Introduction*, Harper, 1961.

One of the best, one of the most recent, and the first popularly priced book to deal comprehensively with the subject. Dr. Harrison is a Professor at Wycliffe College, Toronto, Ont., and has given us the first important contribution from a Canadian.

Howie, Carl G. *The Dead Sea Scrolls and the Living Church*, John Knox, 1958.

Dr. Howie is Pastor of the Calvary Presbyterian Church in San Francisco, and was a student of Dr. Albright at the time of the discovery of the first cave in 1947. He has been to Qumran and has studied in Jerusalem. His book is an admirable introduction for the reader who wants a quick survey without detailed critical notes.

LaSor, William Sanford. *Amazing Dead Sea Scrolls*, Moody Press, 1959.

Dr. LaSor is Professor of Old Testament at Fuller Theological Seminary at Altadena, Calif., and belongs to what is commonly considered to be the extreme conservative wing of Protestantism. This makes the more notable his substantial agreement with Roman Catholic and liberal Protestant scholars on the relations between the scrolls and Christianity. Dr. LaSor is the compiler of the most extensive bibliography of Qumran material to have been published in any language, and edits the "Bibliography" section of the *Revue de Qumran.*

Leaney, A. R. C., Posen, J., and Hanson, R. P. C. *A Guide to the Scrolls: Nottingham Studies on the Qumran Discoveries,* S C M Press Ltd., London, 1958, and Allenson, Naperville, Ill.

Probably the best of the "popular" books on the scrolls to have been published in England. The authors have undertaken to provide an introduction to the discoveries by the Dead Sea and to guide the non-specialist reader to an understanding of the problems that have been raised and the reasons for the positions held by the best scholars.

Milik, J. T. *Ten Years of Discovery in the Wilderness of Judea,* Allenson, 1959.

Father Milik is one of the scholars engaged in the task of editing the scrolls in Jerusalem and he writes from first-hand experience of the discoveries he has helped make.

Murphy, Roland E. *Dead Sea Scrolls and the Bible,* Newman, 1956.

Father Murphy is the head of the Department of Semitic and Egyptian language and literature at the Catholic University of America. This is an informative little book written in an easy and popular style.

Ploeg, Johannes Petrus Maria van der. *Excavations at Qumran,* Longmans, 1958.

162

This is one of the best single-volume books on the scrolls. The Dutch edition, here brilliantly translated, was published in 1956. Father van der Ploeg, a professor at the University of Nijmegen, was one of the first scholars to see the original manuscripts shortly after their discovery. He failed to recognize their antiquity, owing in part to circumstances beyond his control. He makes an *amende honorable* by telling the whole story of the scrolls and discussing their significance for New Testament scholarship.

Stendahl, Krister, ed. *The Scrolls and the New Testament,* Harper, 1957.

A collection of fourteen scholarly articles, drawn for the most part from theological journals, on the relationship of Qumran studies to New Testament scholarship. The articles reflect varying faiths and viewpoints, but achieve an effect of unity. The volume was designed to be an answer to Edmund Wilson's charge that New Testament scholars were afraid to write on this subject.

Sutcliffe, Edmund, S.J. *The Monks of Qumran,* Newman, 1960.

One of the latest and one of the best books available in the English language. Fr. Sutcliffe is particularly good in his discussion of the physical characteristics of the site of the "monastery" and its ability to support a flourishing community. He has also provided an excellent translation of sections of the text.

Yadin, Yigael. *Message of the Scrolls,* Simon and Schuster, 1957.

The best presentation of the story from the Israeli side of the iron curtain. Dr. Yadin is the son of Dr. Sukenik, who procured the first scrolls for the state of Israel. Using his father's diaries, he is able to give a vivid account of the original discovery and purchase. His dating of the scrolls, however, is questioned by many other competent scholars.

Index

OLD TESTAMENT

Leviticus, 19:17, p. 75
  19:17-18, p. 104
Isaiah, 66:9, p. 90 n. 4
Hoseah, 10:12, p. 64
Habakkuk, 2:2, p. 67 n. 5
  2:4, p. 99
Zachariah, 4:14, p. 98
Ecclesiasticus, 23:17, p. 18

NEW TESTAMENT

Matthew, 3:5, pp. 88-89
  3:7, p. 89
  5:33-37, pp. 78-79
  5:43-45, pp. 105-6
  10:9-11, pp. 77-78
  13:24-30, p. 98
  13:37-43, p. 98
  13:47-50, p. 98
  15:2, p. 85
  15:3-20, p. 85
  16:16, p. 131
  18:15-17, pp.74-75
  20:28, p. 112
  21:25-27, p. 89
  22:11-12, p. 93
  23:8, 11, p. 82
  23:37-38, p. 103
  24:5-35, p. 103
  25:31-46, p. 98
  26:26-28, p. 94
  26:28, p. 108
  28:19, p. 89
Mark, 2:27, p. 84
  7:3-4, p. 87, pp. 92-93
Luke, 3:7-14, p. 88
  14:5, p. 84

14:7-11, p. 93
17:3, p. 75
John, 1:3-4, p. 111
  1:14, p. 131
  3:19-21, p. 98
  3:21, p. 105
  4:2, p. 88
  5:8-10, p. 84
  18:36, p. 105
  20:31, p. 100
Acts of the Apostles, 4:12, p. 108
  4:32-35, p. 79
  5:1-11, p. 80
Romans, 1:1-7, p. 100
  1:17, p. 100
  8:2-27, p. 97
II Corinthians, 1:3, p. 110
  6:15, p. 110
Galatians, 3:10-14, p. 100
  3:27-28, p. 82
  4:22-24, p. 102
  6:1, p. 75
Colossians, 1:22, p. 18
  2:11, p. 18
I Timothy, 2:4-6, p. 103
Hebrews, 8:6, p. 102
  8:13, p. 102
  9:15, p. 102
  10:38, p. 100
I John, 4:8, p. 112
Jude, 14, p. 109
Apocalypse, 12, p. 111

ESSENE TEXTS

Rule of the Community, I,3-4,
  p. 104
  I,9-11, pp. 104-5

165

II,4-9, p. 105
II,8, p. 107
II,19-23, p. 93
III,4-6, p. 88
III,6-8, p. 39
III,8, p. 107
III,8-9, p. 88
IV,12-14, p. 104
IV,20-21, p. 39
IV,24-25, p. 97
V,13, p. 87
V,16, p. 85
V,24–VI,1, p. 74
VI,4-6, pp. 89-90
VI,16-17, p. 87
VI,19-20, p. 79
VI,20-21, p. 93 n. 9
VI,22, p. 79
VI,24-25, p. 80
VI,25, p. 87
VII,19-20, p. 93 n. 9
VIII,5-7, p. 107
VIII,10b, p. 107
VIII,15-16, p. 40
IX,3-4, p. 40
IX,4-5, p. 107
IX,8-9, p. 85
IX,10-11, p. 22
X,2-3, p. 36
X,9-17, pp. 153-154
XI,9-10, p. 150
XI,10-15 pp. 153-154
XI,14, p. 108

Rule for the Whole Congrega-
    tion of Israel, I:26, p. 93
II,8-9, p. 84
II,11-22, pp. 90-91
II,12,14,20, p. 22

Collection of Benedictions, II,24,
    p. 41
V,21, p. 103

The War Scroll, I,11-12, p. 62
II,5-6, p. 107
III,9, p. 104

VI,6, p. 102
VII,3, p. 93 n. 11
VII,6, p. 84
IX,5-6, p. 104
IX,7-9, pp. 84-85
XI,7-8, p. 21
XI,8-9, p. 62
XI,13-14, p. 62
XII,1-5, p. 62
XII,13, p. 36
XVII,7-8, pp. 102-3
XVIII,10-11, p. 36
XIX,8, p. 102

Hymns, I,21-23, pp. 149-50
I,26-27, pp. 96-97
II,8-16, pp. 138-39
II;16-19, pp. 137-38
II,19, p. 109
II,20-25, p. 142
II,28-30, p. 142
II;31-36, p. 141
III,7-8, p. 111
III,20-22, p. 97
IV,6, p. 36
IV,8-9, p. 136
IV,16, p. 109
IV,22-27, p. 146
IV,23, p. 36
IV,27-29, p. 147
IV,33-37, pp. 150-51
IV,36-37, p. 107
V,5, p. 136
V,5-6, p. 151
V,6-8, p. 136
V,9-19, pp. 142-43
V,22-25, pp. 136-37
V,28-32, pp. 139-40
V,31-32, p. 36
V,32-37, pp. 134-35
VI,6-8, pp. 146-47
VI,19-22, p. 137
VI,22-25, p. 140
VII,2-5, p. 138
VII,3, p. 36
VII,6-7, p. 40

VII,6-10, pp. 147-48
VII,12-14, pp. 145-46
VII,19-22, p. 148
VII,22-25, pp. 144-45
VII,23-24, p. 36
VIII,4-9, pp. 148-49
VIII,11-12, p. 40
VIII,16, p. 64
VIII,16-17, p. 149
VIII,32-37, p. 135
IX,4-6, pp. 140-41
IX,6-14, pp. 143-44
IX,23-27, p. 145
IX,26, p. 36
IX,29-36, pp. 154-55
IX,31, p. 36
IX,31-32, p. 40
X,14, p. 110
X,5-7, p. 150
XI,26, p. 36
XII,11-13, p. 40
XIII,1, p. 40
XIV,13, p. 40
XIV,17-18, p. 134
XV,24, pp. 106-7
XVI,2, p. 40
XVI,3, p. 40
XVI,7, p. 40
XVI,12, pp. 40-41
XVII,26, p. 41
XVIII,6-7, p. 36

Genesis Commentary, p. 21

Isaiah Commentary, p. 63

Micah Commentary, 8,10; 6,9, p. 68

Nahum Commentary, I,6-8, pp. 51, 55

Habakkuk Commentary, I,13, p. 66
II,1-3, pp. 66-67
II,6-8, p. 67
V,3-5, pp. 60-63
V,9-11, p. 67

V,9-12, p. 50
VII,3-5, p. 67
VIII,1-3, pp. 67, 99, 100
IX,1-2, pp. 17-19, 50-51, 67
IX,9-12, pp. 51, 68
XI,4-8, pp. 33-37, 51, 68

Commentary on Psalm 37, pp. 57-58, 68-69

Damascus Document I,4-5, p. 101
I,9-11, p. 69
I,10-11, p. 45 n. 19
II,4-5, p. 108
II,12-13, pp. 21, 37-41
III,8, p. 64
IV,9-10, p. 108
IV,20–V,2, p. 77
V,11, p. 41
V,21–VI,1, p. 21
VI,2-3, p. 101
VI,10-11, pp. 59, 63-66
VII,4, p. 41
VIII,16-18, p. 101
X,19–XI,17, p. 84
XI,18-20, p. 85
XII,1-2, p. 85
XII,11-17, p. 85
XII,23–XIII,1 pp. 22, 59, 65 n. 12
XIII,2, p. 93
XIV,3-6, p. 93
XIV,19, p. 22
XV,8-10, p. 101
XVI,1-2, pp. 101-102
XIX,10-11, pp. 22, 59
XIX,35–XX,1, pp. 22, 51, 53-54, 59
XX,3, p. 36
XX,6-7, pp. 36-37
XX,13-15, p. 69
XX,14, pp. 51, 53-54, 64
XX,25-26, p. 37
XX,27-34, pp. 69, 99, 100
XX,31-33, p. 69

Book of Enoch, CII,5, p. 18
Collection of Liturgical Prayers, 3, 11, 6-7, p. 41
Unknown work, p. 41

MODERN AUTHORS

Albright, W. F., 1
Allegro, J. M., 10-11, 19-20, 25 n. 15, 26, 27 n. 11, 35, 49, 52-58, 51 n. 3, 51 n. 5, 57 n. 1, 57 n. 2, 63 n. 9, 68 n. 11, 69 n. 14, 70-72, 83, 90 n. 4
Avigad, Nahman, 2 n. 6
Bardtke, H., 115
Barthélemy, D., 2 n. 7, 91 n. 8
Billerbeck, P., 75 n. 3, 93 n. 10
Bory, J.-L., 60
Braun, F. M., 111 n. 9, 111 n. 10
Brown, R. E., 111 n. 9
Burrows, Millar, 2 n. 4, 69 n. 16, 115
Charles, R. H., 28 n. 17
Cowley, A. E., 28 n. 17
Daniélou, Jean, 109 n. 1
Dupont-Sommer, André, 1 n. 2, 2 n. 3, 5-10, 17-20, 19 n. 6, 20 n. 7, 21 n. 8, 21 n. 9, 21 n. 10, 22 n. 11, 24-31, 28 n. 16, 28-35, 33 n. 1, 34 n. 2, 35 n. 4, 35 n. 5, 37-39, 37 n. 10, 39 n. 11, 42, 44-45, 45 n. 19, 46, 46 n. 20, 47, 51 n. 1, 51 n. 2, 58-63, 63 n. 10, 65 n. 12, 67 n. 1, 67 n. 2, 67 n. 7, 70, 86, 92, 100, 100 n. 4, 101 n. 7, 127, 129 n. 1
Étiemble, Professor, 18, 34, 70, 108
Gaster, T. H., 28 n. 17, 62 n. 8, 115
Goosens, R., 19 n. 4, 46 n. 20, 60

Grelot, P., 29, 29 n. 18
Grossouw, W. K. M., 110 n. 5
Grundemann, W., 100 n. 5
Howie, C. G., 70
Jaubert, Annie, 82 n. 9, 82 n. 10, 85 n. 11
Jonge, M. de, 29, 29 n. 18
Kuhn, K. G., 110 n. 5
Laurentin, R., 109 n. 2
Mescerskij, N. A., 47 n. 20
Michel, Amand, 67 n. 7
Milik, J. T., 2 n. 7, 23, 68 n. 9, 71 n. 20
Osty, Emile, 80 n. 5
Pass-Arendzen, J. P., 29 n. 17
Philonenko, M., 18 n. 2, 46 n. 20
Ploeg, J. van der, 94 n. 12
Pontleroy, Michel, 129
Potter, C. F., 13-14, 19, 42-44
Powell Davies, A., 12-13, 92, 95
Renan, Ernst, 5, 7
Roth, C., 157 n. c
Rowley, H. H., 71-72
Schubert, Kurt, 110 n. 6
Skehan, P. W., 71 n. 20
Starcky, Jean, 71 n. 20
Stendahl, Krister, 110 n. 6, 110 n. 9
Strack, H. L., 75 n. 3, 93 n. 10
Strugnell, John, 71 n. 20
Sukenik, E. L., 2 n. 5
Szyszman, S., 47 n. 20
Talmon, Sh., 80 n. 6
Teicher, J. L., 8
Vajda, G., 95
Vaux, Roland de, 1 n. 1, 71 n. 20
Vermes, Geza, 22 n. 11, 156 n. 1
Vogt, Ernest, 110 n. 8
Wilson, Edmund, 12
Yadin, Yigael, 2 n. 6, 22 n. 12, 27 n. 9, 38, 39 n. 13, 90 n. 4